THE CERTIFICATION SERIES

Basic Cruising

The national standard for quality sailing instruction

Published by the UNITED STATES SAILING ASSOCIATION Copyright © 1998 by the UNITED STATES SAILING ASSOCIATION
All rights reserved. No part of this publication may be reproduced, stored in a retrieval system, or transmitted, in any form or by
any means, electronic, mechanical, photocopying, recording, or otherwise without prior written permission from the UNITED
STATES SAILING ASSOCIATION. ISBN 1-882502-27-2. Printed in the United States of America
UNITED STATES SAILING ASSOCIATION P.O. Box 1260, 15 Maritime Drive, Portsmouth, RI 02871

Acknowledgments

Many people have contributed to *Basic Cruising* in many ways. In addition to the superb team of the design director, designer, illustrators, writers, and photographer, there were many generous volunteers and experts who reviewed, edited, and gave technical advice. Special recognition goes to Rob Johnson, Design Director at *SAIL* Magazine, who with great patience and ingenuity assembled all the many pieces from the team and turned them into a book. But none of this could have happened without the support of the Officers and Board of Directors of US SAILING, the Commercial Sailing Committee, the Training Committee, the Safety at Sea Committee, the American Sail Advancement Program (ASAP), sailing schools, and charter companies. We acknowledge and thank them all.

Mark Smith
Designer
A lifelong sailor, graphic designer, editor and illustrator, Mark is currently Director of Marketing for North Sails. Mark was editorial and art director for *Yacht Racing/Cruising* magazine (now *Sailing World*) from 1970-83, editor and publisher of *Sailor* magazine from 1984-86, and editor and art director of *American Sailor* from 1987-89. His works include design and illustration for the *Annapolis Book of Seamanship* by John Rousmaniere and published by Simon and Schuster. Mark lives in Rowayton, CT with his wife Tina and daughters Stephanie, Natalie and Cristina.

Diana Jessie
Writer
Diana enjoys racing and cruising, and has completed a 60,000 mile circumnavigation. Thousands have attended her cruising seminars and read her articles in *SAIL, Sailing, Yachting* and *Yachting World*. At present, she lives and works (on a computer in the quarter berth) aboard her 48-foot sloop in San Francisco Bay. She and her marine surveyor husband Jim are preparing for another long cruise in 1996.

Cover photo courtesy Catalina Yachts

Shimon-Craig Van Collie
Writer
A sailor for the past 30 years, Shimon has cruised and raced the waters of both the East and West coasts. In 1980, he sailed from Hawaii to San Francisco on a 35-foot sloop. In 1993, Shimon and his wife Katrina and son Chai explored Canada's Strait of Georgia on a 30-foot yacht. As a sailing journalist, he's covered sailing and boardsailing since 1979. He is currently the West Coast editor of *Sailing* Magazine and authored the book *Windsurfing: The Call of the Wind*, published in 1992.

Kim Downing
Illustrator
Kim grew up in the Mid-West doing two things, sailing and drawing, so it's only natural that his two favorite pastimes should come together in the production of this book. Kim is the proprietor of MAGAZINE ART and provides technical illustrations to magazine and book publishers. He recently helped his father complete the building of a custom 30-foot sailboat and enjoys racing and daysailing his own boat with his wife and two children.

Rob Eckhardt
Illustrator
A graphic design professional, Rob is currently on the staff of *SAIL* Magazine and has many years of experience as a designer for advertising agencies, publications and his own business clients. He is a graduate of the Rochester Institute of Technology, Rochester, NY. Rob began sailing dinghies as a youngster and currently enjoys one-design racing and coastal cruising.

Chuck Place
Photographer
A professional photographer for seventeen years, Chuck has worked for a wide range of clients, including *National Geographic, Time, Smithsonian, Travel & Leisure* and *SAIL* magazines. Working out of a home base in Santa Barbara, CA, Chuck is able to combine his love for the ocean and images by photographing sailboats, one of his favorite subjects.

Foreword

I was lucky enough to begin sailing the day I was baptized. My childhood summer memories are full of days spent sailing on Lake St. Clair aboard the family's 36-foot classic wooden sailboat. The month of July meant cruising the spectacular North Channel, where we could sail through granite islands that had been cut out by ancient glaciers. Of course, it seemed perfectly natural that there were hundreds of islands (*rocks*) that we could swim to and discover and name for ourselves — such great names as "pool island," "peanut butter island" and its neighbor "jelly island."

Of course, as a child I did not always appreciate the benefits of preparation. Somehow my father had convinced us that sanding the varnish off the 60-foot wooden mast was the easy part and the varnishing was the hard part. So every spring we would give up birthday parties and flute lessons for the "easy" work of sanding.

My parents planned and prepared and saved and took us on a year-long cruise through the Eastern United States and the Bahamas and Caribbean. Through this enlightening experience we realized sailing could take us anywhere in the world. The sailing lifestyle meant freedom.

Since then I have been around the world twice, not to mention the exotic European locales for various regattas.

US SAILING's *Basic Cruising* is the perfect place to start your preparation for many hours of comfortable, safe and enjoyable boating.

Cruising across the lake or through the Southern Ocean requires planning and trust in your boat and your fellow crew members.

With the right training there are no limits for anyone who wants to expand his or her horizons. Good luck and please ENJOY sailing into the sunsets.

Dawn Riley

Dawn Riley has sailed and raced in many parts of the world. Highlights of her many accomplishments include two America's Cup campaigns as America3 team captain on Mighty Mary, the women's entry in 1995, and pitman in the 1992 Cup trials, as well as skipper of the all-women team in the 1993-94 Whitbread Round-the-World Race, and watch captain and engineer of the all-women team in the 1989-90 Whitbread.

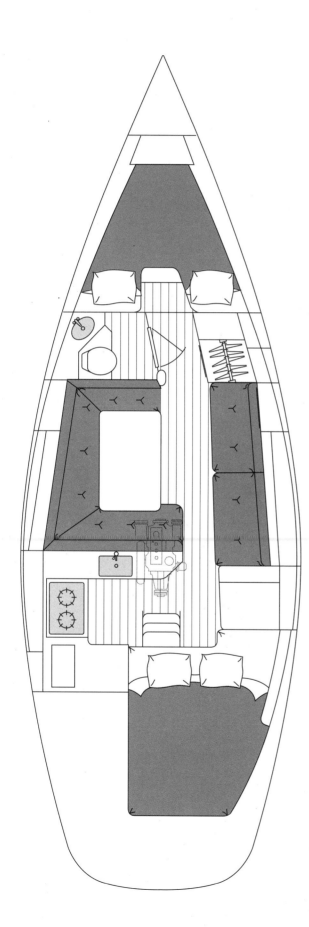

Part 5: Improving Your Skills

Part 6: The Sailing Environment

Part 7: Health, Safety and Emergencies

Appendix

"With repetition come good habits, with good habits comes good seamanship, with good seamanship comes security, and with security comes enjoyment."

John Rousmaniere

The Cruising Mentality

Sailing is to cruising, it could be said, as walking is to backpacking into the woods. In each case, the former is the basic skill upon which the latter activity is based. Like camping on a mountainside, cruising involves many elements, all of which are important to your safety, comfort and enjoyment.

① Seamanship

A good sailor knows more than just the mechanics of sail trim and steering, and good seamanship is more than the ability to perform those tasks. Competent cruising sailors know how to handle the boat and sails in a wide range of wind and sea conditions, skills that require practice and experience.

2 Organization and Planning

Good organization and planning promotes safety and success. Use checklists. Delegate duties among the crew. Have the proper gear on board before leaving the dock. Create a float plan for your trip. Have back up plans and alternatives in case something unexpected happens.

3 Environmental Awareness

While sailing, you need to monitor weather, tides, sea conditions and the movement of other vessels around you. A good sailor knows how to translate and utilize input from the five senses, such as the feel of the wind and the motion of the sea, and how to anticipate potential problems.

4 Safety

Safety afloat prevents accidents. Use the proper equipment for the job. Keep lookouts posted to scan your surroundings. Monitor your electrical, mechanical and other systems for early warning signals. Keep a tidy ship; coiling unused lines, for example, will lessen confusion when something has to be done quickly or under pressure.

5 Teamwork and Communication

Teamwork becomes more important on bigger boats where one person cannot reach everything. The boat's leader (skipper) must communicate effectively in order to maintain the crew's cooperation. Non-verbal techniques, such as hand signals, can be helpful in high winds when it's hard to hear.

6 Anticipation

The sailing environment constantly changes, which requires sailors to be ready to shift gears. Experience will teach you how to anticipate what might happen next, whether it's a change in the wind or a part of the boat that needs attention. Sailors who know what to expect and when to expect it are better equipped than those who don't.

7 Etiquette

Like golf and tennis, certain courtesies have developed over the years in sailing and cruising. The last boat to drop anchor, for example, is the first one to move if the wind changes or current causes two boats to come too close. Minding your manners on the water will enhance your cruising experience.

8 Legal Obligations

Sailboats need to abide by the Navigation Rules. Sailors must also adhere to important federal and state laws and regulations. Oil and plastics, for example, may not be dumped into waters of the United States or offshore. Untreated sewage may not be discharged in lakes or within three miles of the coast. It's against the law to operate a boat while intoxicated. And the use of a VHF radio requires a station license.

"For the true boatman, final satisfaction comes with the harmony of thought and action, of anticipation and response, that makes his craft an extension of his will."

-Norris D. Hoyt

Personal Gear

Your personal comfort can greatly affect your attitude towards sailing and cruising. Wear and use appropriate clothes and gear for the prevailing weather conditions. When cruising, you can be exposed to wind and sun for extended periods, so protect your eyes and skin. The sun's damaging ultraviolet rays penetrate clouds and bounce off the water's surface, so always use a sunscreen with a Sun Protection Factor (SPF) of 15 or higher.

Using **Personal Flotation Devices** (PFDs), or life jackets, is comparable to wearing seat belts in a car; if you've got one on, it can save your life in an emergency. US SAILING recommends that life jackets be worn during classes and especially on cold, windy days.

Type I PFD   **Type II PFD**   **Type III PFD**

The Offshore Life Jacket **(Type I PFD)** is designed to keep an unconscious person's head face up in moderately heavy seas, but is very bulky. The Near-Shore Buoyant Vest **(Type II PFD)** is less bulky, less buoyant and less reliable in turning an unconscious person's face up. The vest **(Type III PFD)** allows the most freedom of movement, both in and out of the water, but is not designed to keep your face out of the water.

Sunglasses protect your eyes from glare. A keeper cord will safeguard against losing your glasses.

A light, knit **cotton shirt** with a collar will keep you cool and protect your upper body from sunburn.

A **water-resistant watch** is useful for keeping track of time and the boat's progress.

Sailing gloves protect your hands, and the cutaway finger tips permit dexterity for delicate tasks.

Long, loose-fitting pants protect your legs from prolonged exposure to the sun and allow freedom of movement.

A **seabag** (below left) is usually made of soft, durable, water-resistant fabric so it can be stowed easily. In addition to foul-weather gear, your bag may contain personal items, such as toiletries, spare clothing, sailing gloves, camera and flashlight.

Deck shoes grip even on wet surfaces and protect you from stubbing your toes on winches and blocks.

Permanently attach a **whistle** and **waterproof light** (see crew's shoulder in illustration) to your cold-weather jacket in case you're separated from the boat.

A **nylon/fleece-lined jacket** with a collar will protect you from wind and spray. For even colder conditions, add additional layers, such as a sweater or turtleneck for more warmth.

A **safety harness** is made of strong webbing with sturdy metal clips. Used properly, it will prevent you from falling overboard and being separated from the boat.

On cold days, **full-fingered sailing gloves** will keep your hands warm while steering and holding lines.

Foul-weather gear offers resistance to wind and water. The chest-high pants can be worn separately or with a jacket. You should have enough room to move freely and be able to wear warm clothes underneath. Velcro or elastic closures at the ankles and wrists will help keep water out. An attached hood will protect your head and neck.

Long underwear worn under **long, loose-fitting pants** will keep your legs warm. Your foul-weather pants can be added as another layer if you need them.

Foul-Weather Gear

Cruising sailors sometimes need protection from high winds, heavy seas and prolonged exposure to chilly weather. Use the layered approach to clothing to adjust for comfort. Wool and modern synthetics like polypropylene provide warmth even when wet. And don't forget to protect your extremities with hats, gloves and warm socks.

Protect the top of your head from heat loss. Wear a waterproof hat with a brim to keep your head dry and warm. A knit ski cap under your foul-weather jacket hood will help keep you warm as well.

Sea boots provide extra protection for your lower legs. They should be worn with a **PFD** because boots impede your movement if you fall overboard.

Parts of the Hull

Cruising keelboats differ from daysailing keelboats in a few ways. They are more spacious and equipped with an engine and propeller, wheel steering in some cases, and cooking and sleeping accommodations. Here are some familiar terms plus some new ones.

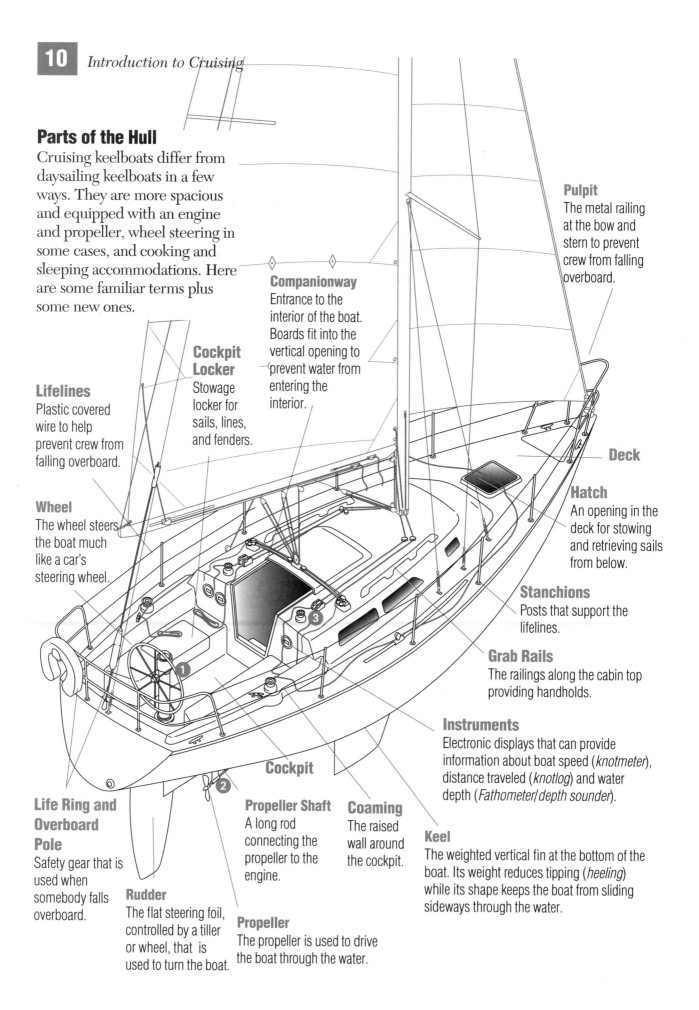

Companionway
Entrance to the interior of the boat. Boards fit into the vertical opening to prevent water from entering the interior.

Pulpit
The metal railing at the bow and stern to prevent crew from falling overboard.

Cockpit Locker
Stowage locker for sails, lines, and fenders.

Lifelines
Plastic covered wire to help prevent crew from falling overboard.

Wheel
The wheel steers the boat much like a car's steering wheel.

Deck

Hatch
An opening in the deck for stowing and retrieving sails from below.

Stanchions
Posts that support the lifelines.

Grab Rails
The railings along the cabin top providing handholds.

Instruments
Electronic displays that can provide information about boat speed (*knotmeter*), distance traveled (*knotlog*) and water depth (*Fathometer/depth sounder*).

Cockpit

Life Ring and Overboard Pole
Safety gear that is used when somebody falls overboard.

Propeller Shaft
A long rod connecting the propeller to the engine.

Coaming
The raised wall around the cockpit.

Keel
The weighted vertical fin at the bottom of the boat. Its weight reduces tipping (*heeling*) while its shape keeps the boat from sliding sideways through the water.

Rudder
The flat steering foil, controlled by a tiller or wheel, that is used to turn the boat.

Propeller
The propeller is used to drive the boat through the water.

The pedestal **1** includes the wheel for steering the boat, the compass, and the throttle and gear shift controls for the engine.

The cabin top **3** may have winches, cleats, and stoppers for sail trim as well as grab rails.

The propeller is attached to a propeller shaft **2** which passes through a fitting (*shaft seal, stuffing box, or packing gland*) in the hull. This fitting should be inspected regularly. This propeller shaft also has a vertical support, called a *strut*.

This is a through-hull fitting viewed from outside the boat and is located below the waterline. Through-hull fittings with valves (*seacocks*) allow water to flow in or drain out from the sinks, toilet (*head*), engine and bilge.

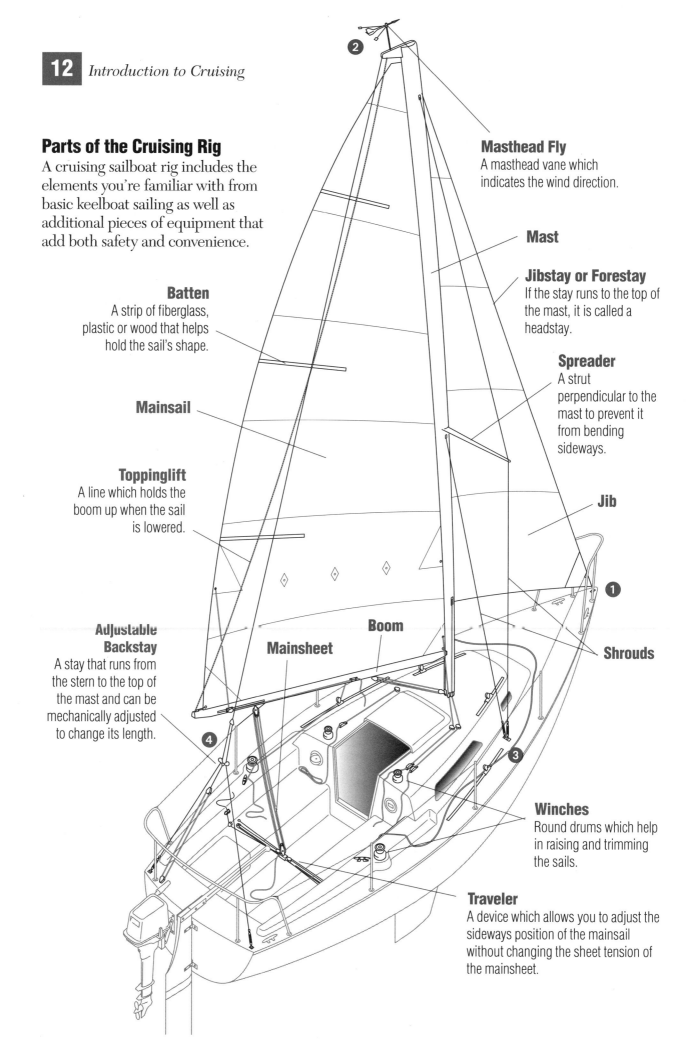

Parts of the Cruising Rig

A cruising sailboat rig includes the elements you're familiar with from basic keelboat sailing as well as additional pieces of equipment that add both safety and convenience.

Masthead Fly
A masthead vane which indicates the wind direction.

Mast

Jibstay or Forestay
If the stay runs to the top of the mast, it is called a headstay.

Spreader
A strut perpendicular to the mast to prevent it from bending sideways.

Jib

Shrouds

Batten
A strip of fiberglass, plastic or wood that helps hold the sail's shape.

Mainsail

Toppinglift
A line which holds the boom up when the sail is lowered.

Adjustable Backstay
A stay that runs from the stern to the top of the mast and can be mechanically adjusted to change its length.

Mainsheet

Boom

Winches
Round drums which help in raising and trimming the sails.

Traveler
A device which allows you to adjust the sideways position of the mainsail without changing the sheet tension of the mainsheet.

These pulleys (*blocks*) are part of the adjustable backstay ❹. Pulling down on the blocks tightens the backstay which bends the mast and changes the shape of the mainsail.

This is the drum of the roller furling system ❶ which allows you to stow the jib by wrapping it around the headstay.

At the masthead ❷, the halyards run over a pulley (*sheave*) at the top of the mast and then down to the deck.

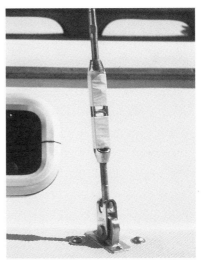

The shroud length can be adjusted at deck level by a mechanical device called a turnbuckle ❸, which can be tightened or loosened. The turnbuckles are secured with pins, and the tape covering them protects you and the sails from rips or tears.

Parts of the Interior

The interior of the boat is a compact living area providing the essential comforts of home. Good interior layout is important to cruising comfort.

Head

The bathroom is called the head and contains a sink and toilet (Marine Sanitation Device or MSD in U.S. Coast Guard vocabulary). Some heads also have showers.

Saloon

This seating area doubles as sleeping and eating spaces. A folding or drop-down table converts this area into a sleeping space.

Galley

Your on board kitchen includes a gimballed stove, a sink, and icebox or refrigerator. Locker space (cupboards) holds dishes, cookware, utensils and provisions.

Forepeak

The area of the boat which contains a chain locker for the anchor.

Forward Cabin

This area contains a vee-berth, a bed for two which narrows at the forward end.

Hanging Locker

A small closet for clothes.

Settee Berth

This seat also serves as a berth.

Sole

The floor of the cabin. Removable floorboards provide access to the area (*bilge*) underneath.

Engine Compartment

The engine is located under the galley counter on this boat. Other boats may have it behind the companionway steps.

Navigation Station

All equipment pertinent to navigation and weather are stored in this area in or near the chart table.

Quarter Berth

The aft (rear) berth is located under the cockpit area adjacent to the navigation station.

IMPORTANT ITEMS

You should always know where to find:

▶ **fire extinguishers** - near galley and engine compartment

▶ **bilge pumps** (manual and electrical) - cockpit, bilge

▶ **seacocks** - head, galley, engine compartment

▶ **master battery switch and electrical panel** - near navigation station

▶ **stove fuel shutoff** - near the stove and at the tank

▶ **life jackets** - various locations

Photo courtesy of Catalina Yachts

This is a view looking forward on a small cruising boat. The table can be lowered to convert into a vee-berth **4**.

The saloon **1** is viewed looking toward the forward cabin with the galley sinks and dining area on the left (*port*) side. Attached to the overhead is a grab rail to use when sailing upwind or in windy conditions.

The chart table **3** opens for stowing charts, rulers, dividers, and other navigation equipment.

The galley **2** is compact with sinks, a two-burner stove and cupboards located above it. Openings in the countertop access the icebox or refrigerator and other lockers.

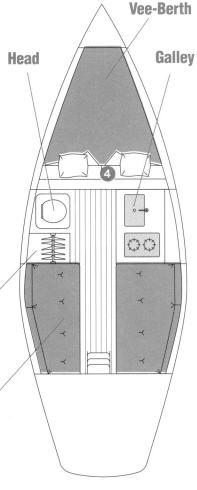

Vee-Berth

Head

Galley

Hanging Locker

Settee Berth

The interior of a small cruising boat

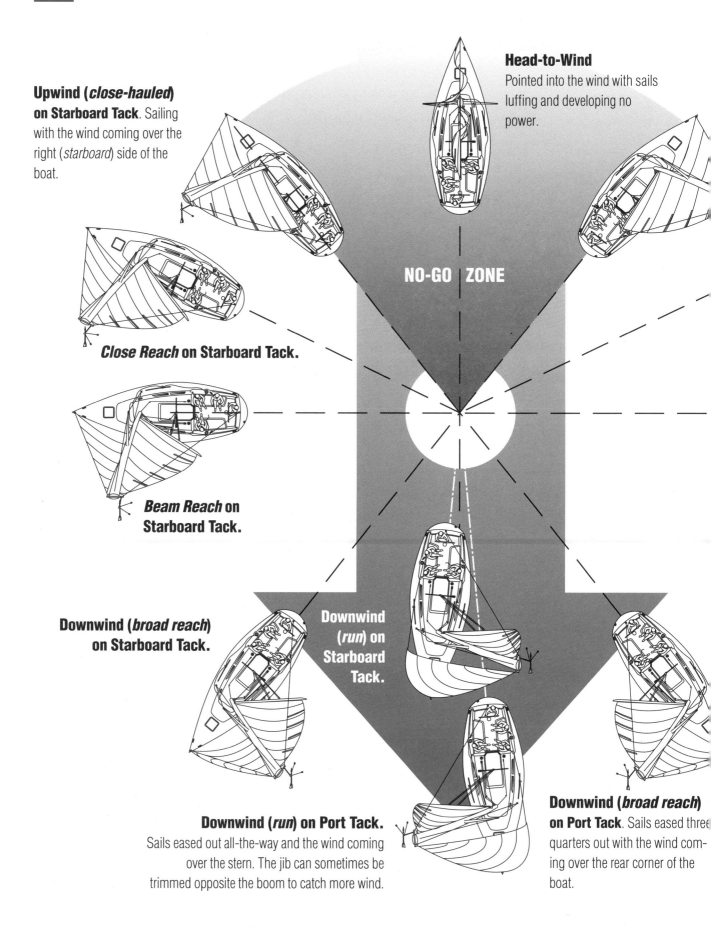

Upwind (*close-hauled*) on Starboard Tack. Sailing with the wind coming over the right (*starboard*) side of the boat.

Head-to-Wind
Pointed into the wind with sails luffing and developing no power.

NO-GO ZONE

Close Reach **on Starboard Tack.**

Beam Reach **on Starboard Tack.**

Downwind (*broad reach*) on Starboard Tack.

Downwind (*run*) on Starboard Tack.

Downwind (*broad reach*) on Port Tack. Sails eased three quarters out with the wind coming over the rear corner of the boat.

Downwind (*run*) on Port Tack.
Sails eased out all-the-way and the wind coming over the stern. The jib can sometimes be trimmed opposite the boom to catch more wind.

Upwind (*close-hauled*)

on Port Tack. Sailing as close to the wind as possible with the wind coming over the left (*port*) side of the boat.

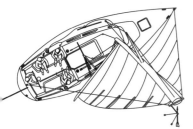

Close Reach on Port Tack.

Sails slightly eased with the wind coming over the left, forward part of the boat.

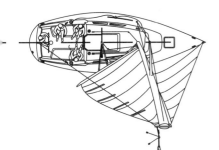

Beam Reach on Port Tack.

Sails eased halfway out with the wind coming perpendicular to the centerline of the boat.

The masthead fly points to the direction of the wind relative to the boat's heading.

Points of Sail

Sailors have a special vocabulary for the different sailing directions that a boat assumes relative to the wind. Here's your "dictionary" for those terms.

The wind instruments provide a deck-level readout of wind direction and velocity.

Sailboat Dynamics

A sailboat is a wonderful combination of balancing forces. One of the most important is the sideways force resulting from the wind acting on the sails and rig. Opposing this force is the sideways resistance to the water offered by the keel and underwater part of the hull. (See illustration below.)

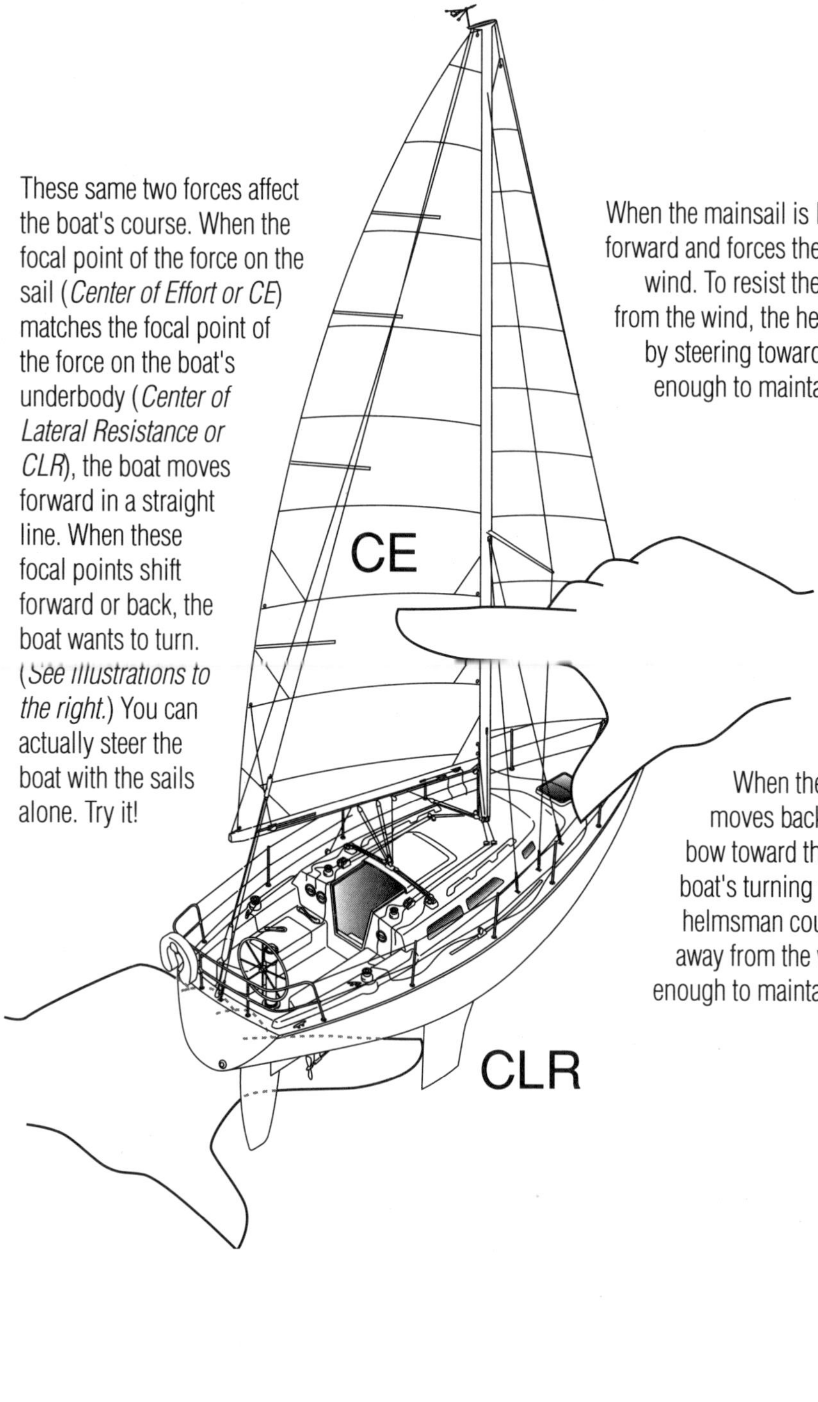

Balanced
The opposing forces of wind (*CE*) and water (*CLR*) are balanced and the boat moves forward.

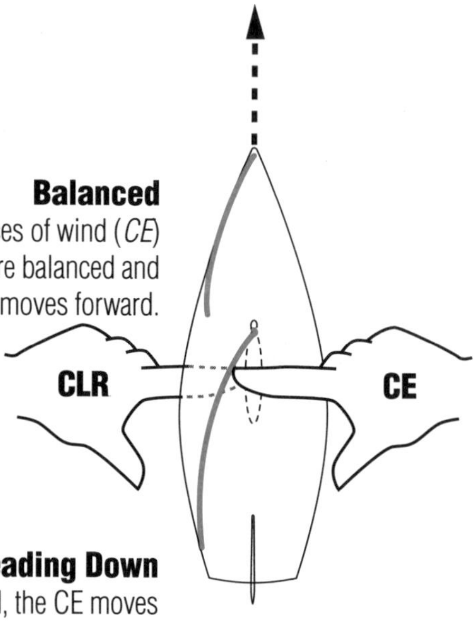

CLR   **CE**

These same two forces affect the boat's course. When the focal point of the force on the sail (*Center of Effort or CE*) matches the focal point of the force on the boat's underbody (*Center of Lateral Resistance or CLR*), the boat moves forward in a straight line. When these focal points shift forward or back, the boat wants to turn. (*See illustrations to the right.*) You can actually steer the boat with the sails alone. Try it!

Heading Down
When the mainsail is luffed, the CE moves forward and forces the bow away from the wind. To resist the boat's turning away from the wind, the helmsman counteracts by steering toward the wind (*lee helm*) enough to maintain a straight course.

CE

CLR

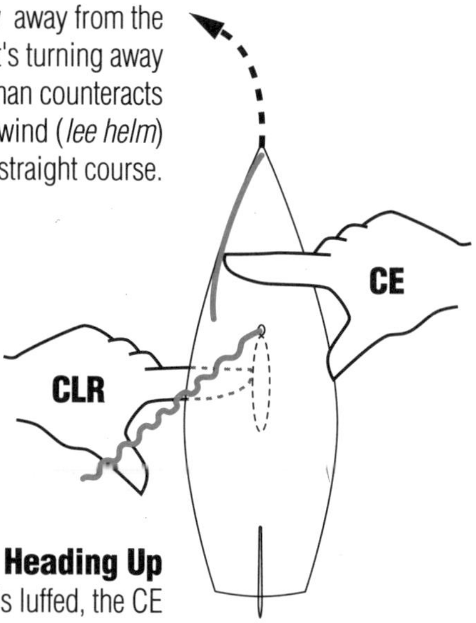

Heading Up
When the jib is luffed, the CE moves backward and forces the bow toward the wind. To resist the boat's turning toward the wind, the helmsman counteracts by steering away from the wind (*weather helm*) enough to maintain a straight course.

CE

CLR

CLR   **CE**

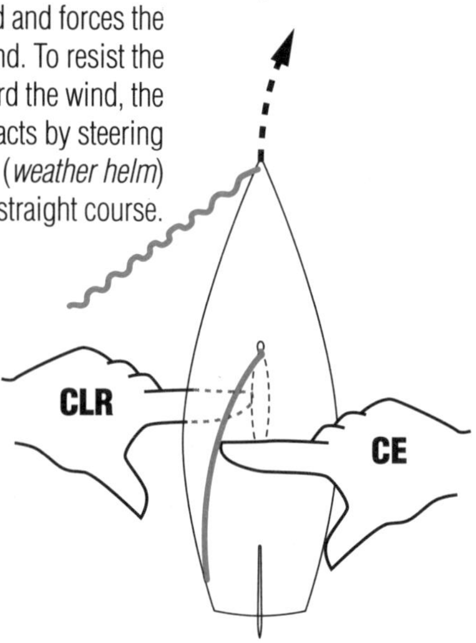

Apparent Wind

The wind you feel on your face while sailing is a combination of the true wind that's blowing across the water and the wind created by the boat's forward motion. The combination of these two winds is called the apparent wind. This is the wind you see indicated by the masthead fly and the telltales on the shrouds, and to which you adjust your sails.

True Wind.

If your boat was stationary on the water, the only wind you would feel would be the true wind.

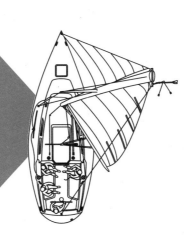

True Wind

Wind Created by Boat's Motion.

Like riding a bicycle or a car, your movement creates a breeze that comes from directly in front.

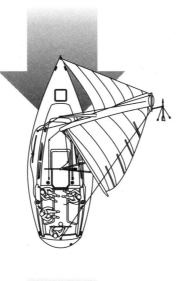

Apparent Wind.

The combination of true wind and wind created by the boat's motion is the apparent wind.

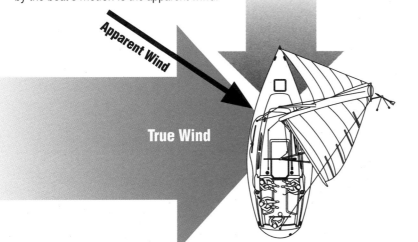

Apparent Wind

True Wind

Getting There and Returning

Cruising on a sailboat usually means sailing to a destination and returning to your home port. This usually involves the basic maneuvers. You'll sail long stretches toward the wind (*upwind or close-hauled*), across the wind (*reaching*) and with the wind (*broad reach or a run*). At times, you'll zig-zag at right angles toward the wind (*tacking*) and zig-zag at various angles with the wind (*jibing*).

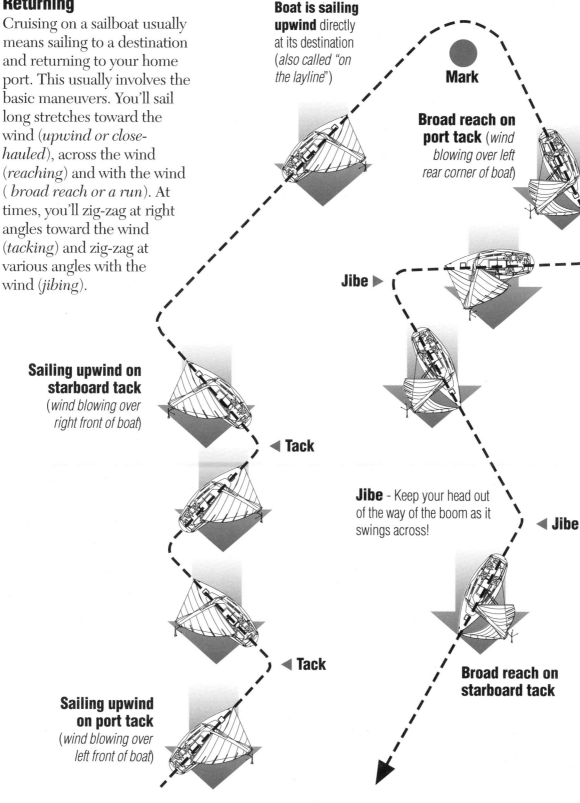

Boat is sailing upwind directly at its destination (*also called "on the layline"*)

Mark

Broad reach on port tack (*wind blowing over left rear corner of boat*)

Jibe ▶

Sailing upwind on starboard tack (*wind blowing over right front of boat*)

◀ Tack

Jibe - Keep your head out of the way of the boom as it swings across!

◀ Jibe

◀ Tack

Broad reach on starboard tack

Sailing upwind on port tack (*wind blowing over left front of boat*)

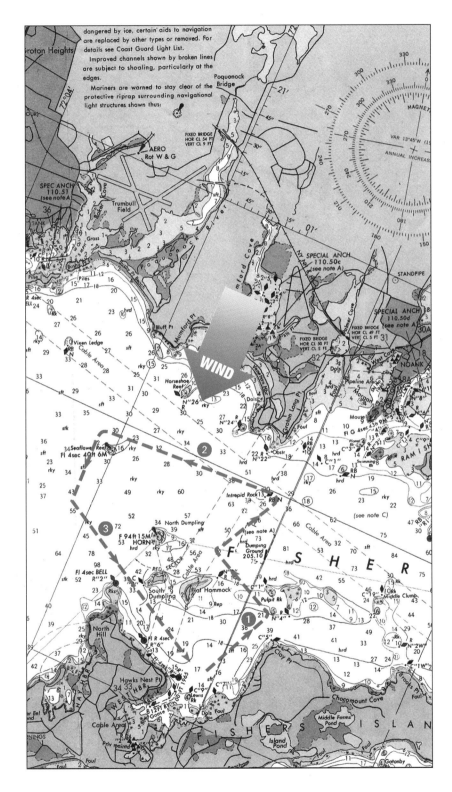

Getting There and Returning

The short cruise shown on the chart uses the following basic sailing maneuvers: **①** leaving West Harbor, sail upwind to the buoy marking Intrepid Rock, tacking twice to pass between the buoys off Pulpit Rock and Flat Hammock; **②** then sail across the wind on a beam reach around Seaflower Reef; **③** return to West Harbor sailing downwind and jibing to pass between South Dumpling and the bell buoy off North Hill. You can plan trips and keep track of your progress by using a chart.

The post (lubber's line) on the forward side of your compass marks the direction (heading) toward which the boat is pointing. Each time you change direction, make it a habit to note your new heading on the compass as well as the time on your watch.

Sailing with a Compass

You can use your compass to see what heading (*direction*) you're sailing or to sail a predetermined heading. If you plan to sail from A to B, you can determine the compass heading by drawing a line on the compass rose parallel to the line between A and B. Read the heading (275°) where the line goes through the inner ring of the compass rose (*circled below*).

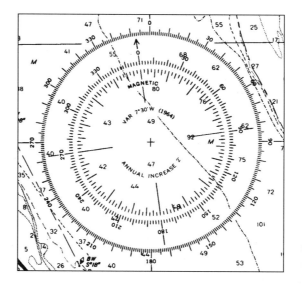

Compass Rose

Use the compass rose to relate your boat's compass heading (*direction*) to a chart or to determine the course you want to steer. The outer ring of the rose is degrees relative to the geographic or true north pole. The inner ring is oriented to magnetic north. Use the inner ring because your compass indicates magnetic degrees.

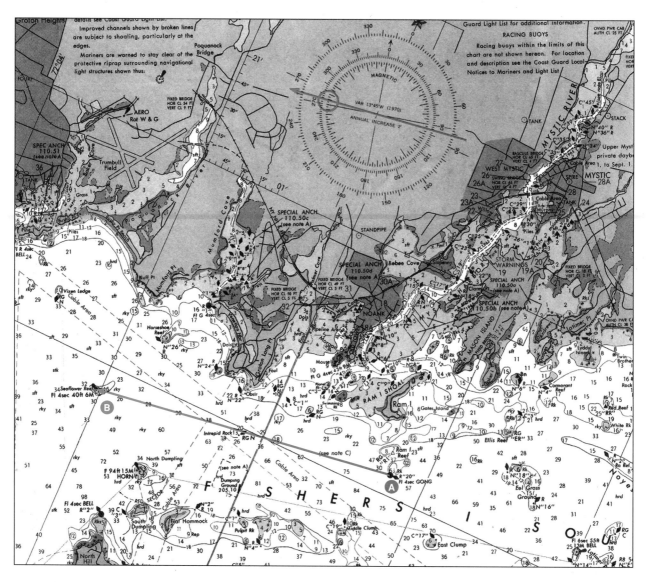

Taking Bearings

You can see objects on the shore while you sail from A to B and by using your compass you can determine the object's bearing (*direction*) from the boat. The bearings for the stack and old tower have been taken and transferred to the chart.

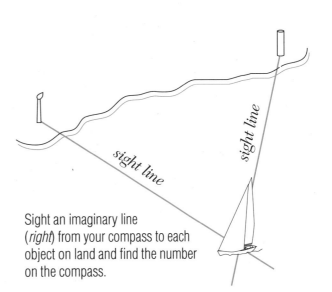

The compass bearings for the stack and old tower are drawn on the compass rose from which the imaginary sight lines, or bearings, are reproduced on the chart. Their intersection indicates the position of the boat.

Sight an imaginary line (*right*) from your compass to each object on land and find the number on the compass.

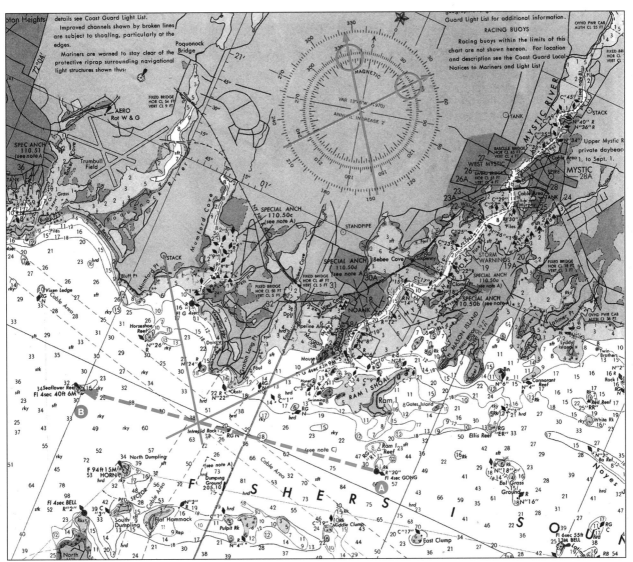

Using the Engine

Cruising boats are equipped with auxiliary engines, which drive the boat by means of a propeller. Boats usually motor along with sails down, but they can "motorsail" with the mainsail up. When powering, remember that a line in the water can wrap around the propeller, disabling the engine. Make a habit of checking lines before starting the engine.

Engine controls are located close to the steering station so the helmsman can operate the throttle and gear shift.

The turning propeller moves the boat. The path of the propeller moving through the water resembles a spiral like a giant corkscrew.

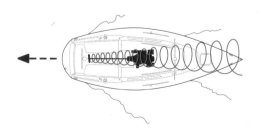

When the gear is shifted into reverse, the propeller turns in the opposite direction driving the boat backward.

When the engine is in forward gear, the propeller rotates and drives the boat forward.

Propeller Types

Most boats have propellers with fixed blades, but some blades may fold or swivel.

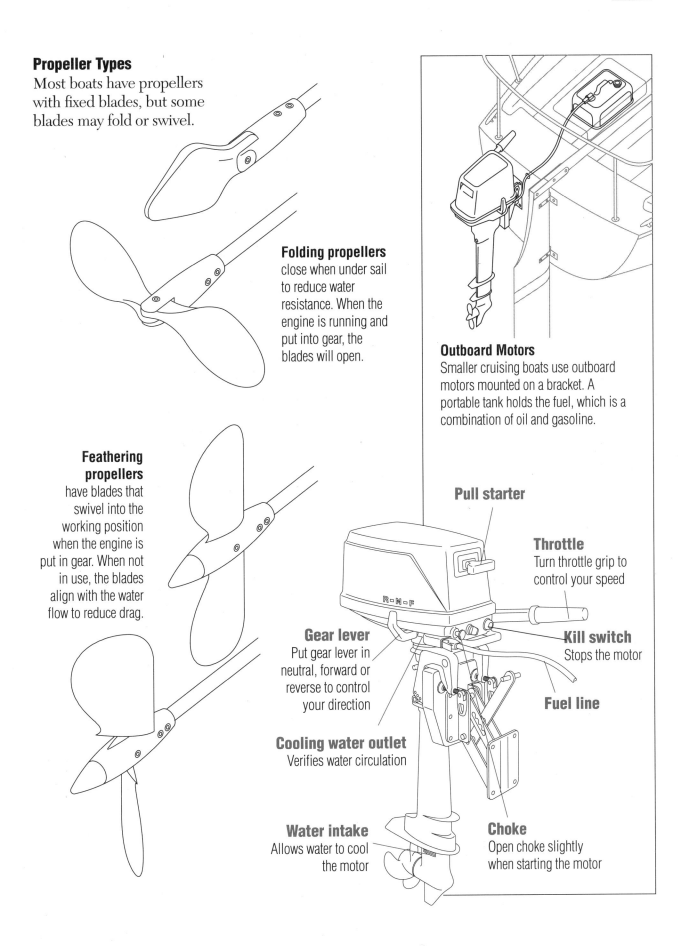

Folding propellers close when under sail to reduce water resistance. When the engine is running and put into gear, the blades will open.

Feathering propellers have blades that swivel into the working position when the engine is put in gear. When not in use, the blades align with the water flow to reduce drag.

Outboard Motors
Smaller cruising boats use outboard motors mounted on a bracket. A portable tank holds the fuel, which is a combination of oil and gasoline.

Pull starter

Throttle
Turn throttle grip to control your speed

Gear lever
Put gear lever in neutral, forward or reverse to control your direction

Kill switch
Stops the motor

Fuel line

Cooling water outlet
Verifies water circulation

Water intake
Allows water to cool the motor

Choke
Open choke slightly when starting the motor

Engine Systems

There are several types of auxiliary power used in sailboats including outboard motors, and diesel or gasoline engines. Because diesel engines are safer, they are found in most cruising boats with inboard power. Gasoline fumes can collect in the bilge and explode when ignited, whereas diesel fumes are not explosive.

Engines require several ingredients to operate.

▶ Fuel carried in clean tanks and kept clean by filters.

▶ Oil to lubricate the engine.

▶ Coolant and cooling water to prevent overheating.

▶ Fresh air circulating through vents and cleaned by filters.

▶ A charged starting battery to activate the starter motor.

❶ **Fuel tank opening** with a cap (*deck plate*) is marked "fuel" where fuel can be pumped into the tank.

❷ **Fuel tank** is equipped with a vent to allow air to escape outside the boat when filling the tank.

❸ **Raw-water intake** system provides seawater to mix with the exhaust gases to cool and expel them from the boat through the exhaust system.

❹ **Seacock** allows raw-water (*seawater*) to flow in.

❺ **Raw-water filter** strains and collects debris from the raw-water (*seawater*).

❻ **Lift can** combines raw-water (*seawater*) with exhaust gases to cool engine exhaust.

❼ **Anti-siphon loop** and drain tube break the suction so water can't flow back into the engine.

❽ **Exhaust outlet** is working properly when water flows out. If there is no water, turn off the engine immediately and check raw-water intake system. Check whether seacock is open and filter is clean.

❾ **Alternator** generates electricity to charge the batteries.

❿ **Batteries** provide the electricity for lights, instruments, and starting the engine.

⓫ **Fuel filter** collects impurities.

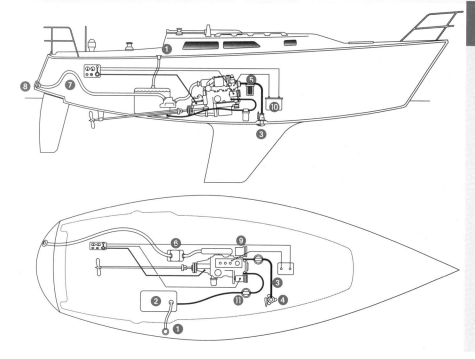

INBOARD STARTING CHECKLIST

▶ Complete the engine inspection on following page.

▶ Turn battery switch to ON position.

▶ Start engine blower (if gasoline)

▶ Set engine stop control (*kill lever*) to the operate position.

▶ Put gear lever in neutral; throttle slightly open.

▶ Preheat (if diesel) and start engine.

▶ Check exhaust outlet for water within 30 seconds of starting.

Engine Inspection

Regularly look for wear and changes in the engine condition. Visual inspection tells you about each of the systems.

ENGINE INSPECTION CHECKLIST

- ▶ Fuel filters collect impurities and should be changed regularly.
- ▶ Oil dipstick indicates correct oil level and condition.
- ▶ Raw-water filter must be clean.
- ▶ Raw-water seacock should be easy to open.
- ▶ Cooling fluid should be topped and clean.

- ▶ Belts need to fit snuggly to turn pumps and alternators and run compressors.
- ▶ Transmission fluid should be checked periodically.
- ▶ Engine controls need to operate freely.

Fueling

Make sure fuel is added only through the deck plate marked "fuel" or "diesel" and there are no open flames in the area. Monitor the fuel flow continuously and wipe up any fuel spilled on deck. Do not hose spilled fuel overboard. Secure the deck plate when finished.

Checking gauges

When the engine is running, don't forget to check the oil pressure and water temperature gauges periodically. Some boats have alarm lights and buzzers to warn you if dangerous conditions exist.

Cooling water

Remove the cap ONLY when the engine is cool to check cooling fluid level and condition.

Seacock

The through-hull seacock for the raw-water intake must be open.

Raw-water intake

The raw-water intake filter should be free of grass, plastic and aquatic life that could clog the system.

OUTBOARD STARTING CHECKLIST

1. Secure tilt control lever in down position.
2. Check for adequate fuel in tank.

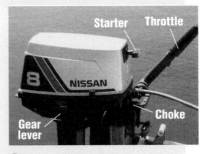

3. Open fuel tank vent.
4. Check that both ends of fuel line are securely attached.
5. Pump bulb until firm.
6. Put gear lever in neutral.
7. Pull choke out.
8. Put throttle in start position.
9. Pull starter.
10. Check cooling water outlet.
11. Push choke in after engine starts.

MSD (Head) System

The toilet (*head*) is part of the Marine Sanitation Device (*MSD*). Proper use and regular inspection of the entire MSD is essential to your cruising comfort. Always explain the operation of the head to your crew to avoid unpleasant mistakes. The head is connected to a holding tank because Federal Regulations prohibit pumping waste overboard, unless you are more than three miles offshore in the ocean. Raw-water (*seawater*) comes into the head for flushing and the discharge flows into the holding tank by using the manual double action pump. The holding tank can be emptied at pumpout stations frequently located at marinas.

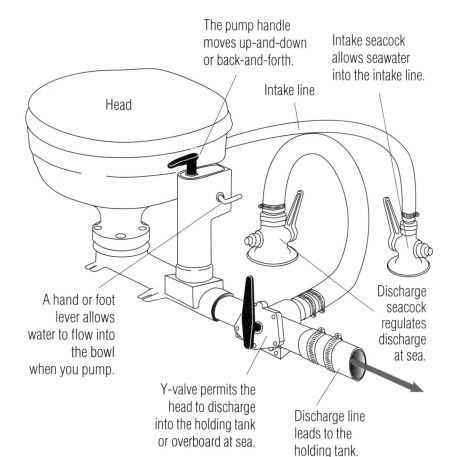

The pump handle moves up-and-down or back-and-forth.

Intake seacock allows seawater into the intake line.

Intake line

Head

A hand or foot lever allows water to flow into the bowl when you pump.

Y-valve permits the head to discharge into the holding tank or overboard at sea.

Discharge line leads to the holding tank.

Discharge seacock regulates discharge at sea.

Holding tank

Seacocks

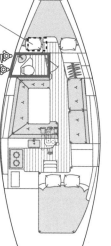

Small cruising boats may have a portable head which has a built-in holding tank. The whole unit is carried off the boat to be emptied.

HEAD OPERATION CHECKLIST

1. Open raw-water (*seawater*) seacock.
2. Open valve to holding tank.
3. Depress hand or foot lever and pump a small amount of water into bowl before using.
4. Depress hand or foot lever to flush, and pump until bowl is clear. Then pump additional strokes to make sure the discharge line is clear.
5. Release hand or foot lever and pump bowl dry.
6. Close all valves and seacock after use.

Do's and Don'ts

▶ Never pump a head with the valves or seacock closed. If this happens, you will feel resistance while pumping. Stop immediately and check valves and seacock.

▶ Close all valves and seacock after using.

▶ Don't put anything in the head except a small amount of toilet paper or something that has been swallowed first.

▶ Leave the bowl and toilet clean for the next person.

Electrical System

Starting the auxiliary engine and using lights and instruments are dependent upon electricity. Knowing the location of the wiring, how to inspect the battery, and the operation of the battery switch demand little effort and offer great rewards. The electrical system on most boats is 12 volt DC.

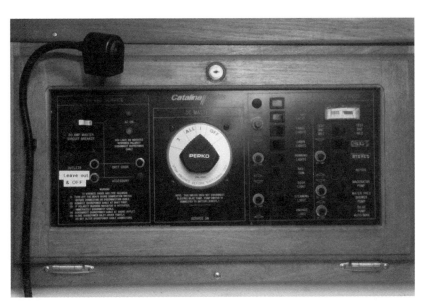

The battery switch and a series of labeled switches are located on the electrical control panel. Most cruising boats are equipped with switches for navigation lights and interior lights. Electronic instruments, radios and other equipment may also be listed on the control panel.

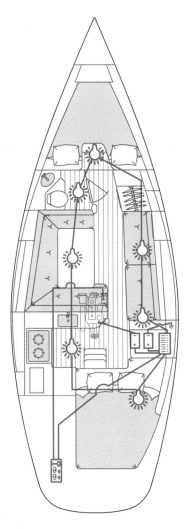

BATTERY CHECKLIST

1. Locate the batteries and check the fluid levels.
2. Make sure the batteries are clean with no signs of corrosion.
3. Set battery switch to the position you want (1,2, or ALL) before starting the engine or turning on lights.
4. Set the battery switch to ALL if you know the batteries are low. This may provide sufficient power to start the engine.
5. Determine if your automatic bilge pump is wired separately from the battery switch.

Shore power outlets on cruising boats provide electricity for charging the battery.

Don'ts

▶ Don't change the position of the battery switch while the engine is running.

▶ Don't leave switches in the ON position when you leave the boat.

▶ Don't overcharge the batteries. Read manufacturer information.

The typical cruising boat (*above*) is wired to carry electricity to the locations in the diagram. Usually, the batteries are located near the engine. One battery is designated for starting the engine and the other is used for the "house" to operate instruments and lights. On the battery switch they are designated as battery one and battery two. The ALL designation means both batteries are on.

Fresh Water System

Boats carry a limited amount of fresh water. Check the quality and quantity of water the tanks hold, because you use it for drinking, cooking and washing. Small boats have a manual pressure system which you pump with your hand or foot to bring water into the sink. Bigger boats have the manual system as well as a pressure system which operates with faucets like the one in your home.

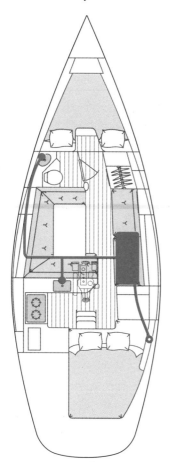

In the boat above, there is a water tank under the starboard settee. Before sailing, locate the deck plate and places where water is used on board.

Big boats often have a pressure water system (top) with faucets and a manual pump system (bottom) at the same sink.

FRESH WATER CHECKLIST

1. Run the water hose for 30 seconds to clear debris before filling.
2. Taste the water to check quality.
3. Close sink and basin faucets so water doesn't run out during filling.
4. Check the deck plate to see it's labeled "water" before filling.
5. After filling, tighten deck plate securely so the water tank is not contaminated by seawater or water used to clean the deck.
6. If the pressure water pump is running constantly, check the faucets and system for leaks and check the water tank. The pump will run continuously and burn out if the water tank is empty.

The manual water pump can be a hand pump or a foot pump. Foot pumps let you use both hands while pumping.

There are several deck plates on most boats. Be sure you fill the one marked "water," not "waste" or "fuel." The filler cap is threaded and screws into the deck plate.

Sumps

The sump is a cavity or tank in the bilge into which water drains. Boats with showers usually have sumps, which are emptied overboard by a sump pump. The sump needs to be inspected and cleaned regularly because debris and hair will clog the pump intake. Boats without sumps drain waste water directly into the bilge.

Bilge System

Never let the bilge be "out of sight, out of mind." A regular visual inspection of the bilge should become a habit. You will quickly learn what is normal water in the bilge - rain water coming down the mast, ice box drainage and the drip from the stuffing box - and recognize water that indicates a problem. Check the bilge regularly.

Many boats have a manual bilge pump which can be operated on deck. Be sure that you can access the handle and that the pump is operating before sailing.

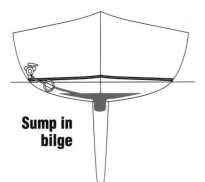

Sump in bilge

The screen on the bilge pump intake will clog with debris. Inspect and clean it regularly.

CHECKLIST

1. Locate bilge pump handles for manually-operated systems and switches for electric pumps.
2. Check the bilge pump switch at the electrical control panel and the bilge alarm. Automatic bilge pumps are not wired through the battery switch so they are active even when the boat is unattended.
3. Check all bilge pump intake screens to be sure they are free of debris.
4. Inspect each through-hull fitting for a working valve.
5. Look for wooden plugs at each through-hull fitting.

Each through-hull fitting should be clearly labeled identifying its use. There should be a wooden plug at each through-hull fitting that can be used in emergencies.

Tips

▶ For salt water sailors, taste the water in the bilge if you aren't sure whether it is coming from a leak or rain water.

▶ If an electric bilge pump is set on automatic, it can run your battery down pumping water from an undetected leak. An automatic pump should have an alarm.

Sail Controls

The running rigging, which includes the sheets and halyards and their pulleys, controls and adjusts the sails. The running rigging also includes the sail shaping controls such as the outhaul and boom vang.

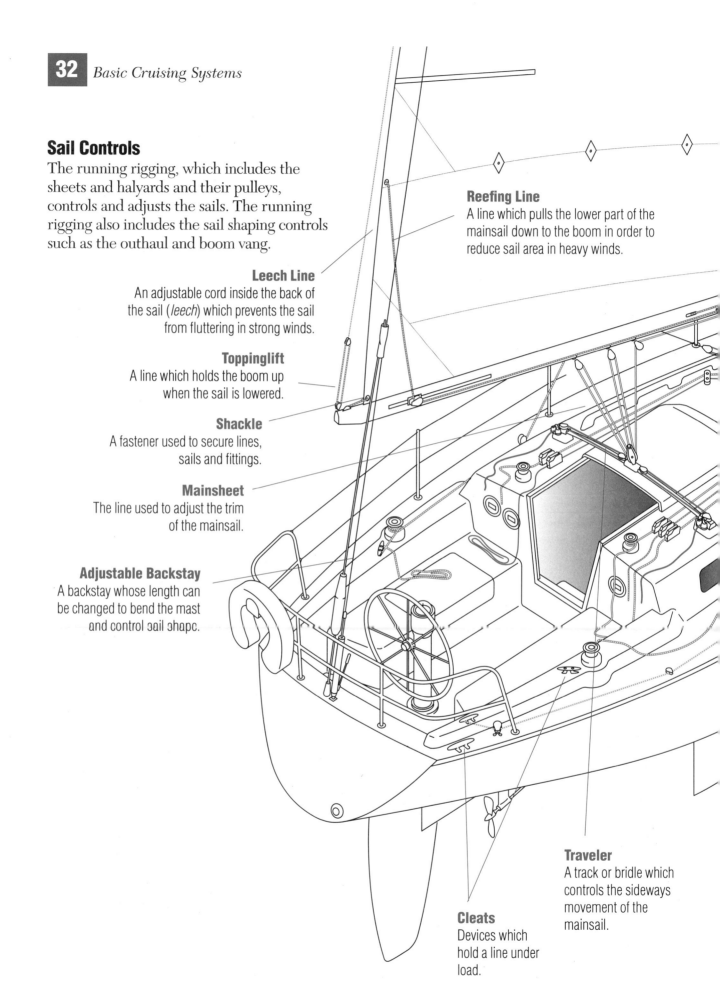

Reefing Line
A line which pulls the lower part of the mainsail down to the boom in order to reduce sail area in heavy winds.

Leech Line
An adjustable cord inside the back of the sail (*leech*) which prevents the sail from fluttering in strong winds.

Toppinglift
A line which holds the boom up when the sail is lowered.

Shackle
A fastener used to secure lines, sails and fittings.

Mainsheet
The line used to adjust the trim of the mainsail.

Adjustable Backstay
A backstay whose length can be changed to bend the mast and control sail shape.

Traveler
A track or bridle which controls the sideways movement of the mainsail.

Cleats
Devices which hold a line under load.

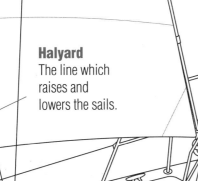

Halyard
The line which raises and lowers the sails.

Cunningham
A line which controls the tension on the front part of the mainsail and affects the shape of the sail.

Halyards can be led to special cleats called line stoppers, which can be released fairly easily under load.

Outhaul
The line which pulls the foot of the sail out on the boom.

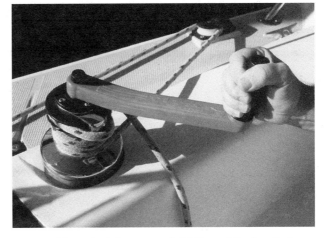

A self-tailing winch has a special fitting at the top that grabs the line while you turn the winch handle.

Boom Vang
A block and tackle or adjustable hydraulic tube which holds the boom down and controls the tension on the back edge of the mainsail (*leech*).

Jib Fairlead
A fitting which leads the jib sheet back to a cleat in the cockpit.

A winch is a revolving drum which helps pull in and hold sheets and halyards. The friction of the line on the drum reduces the pull you feel as you trim. A winch handle gives you more mechanical advantage for lines under heavy load.

Jib sheets are led to the deck, where they pass through a fitting (*jib fairlead*). Many boats have tracks to slide the fairleads back and forth for different size jibs and wind conditions.

Weather

Newspapers, radio, television, telephone, and VHF radio forecasts keep sailors informed about predicted wind speed and direction, and storm possibilities.

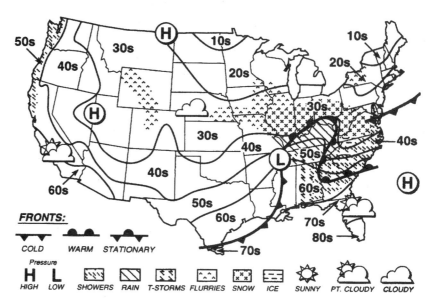

FRONTS:
COLD   WARM   STATIONARY

Pressure
H L   SHOWERS   RAIN   T-STORMS   FLURRIES   SNOW   ICE   SUNNY   PT. CLOUDY   CLOUDY
HIGH LOW

Weather maps help you predict what kind of weather to expect on the water. High pressure systems (H) usually indicate good, mild weather, while low pressure systems (L) usually are accompanied by a warm or cold front and inclement weather.

Cumulus clouds, which are large, white, and fluffy, are often an indicator of good weather.

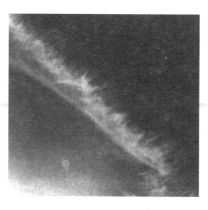

Wispy, thin **cirrus clouds** usually mean good weather for the day, but may be a prediction that a change in weather is on the way.

Low layered **stratus clouds** usually bring steady rain.

Towering **cumulonimbus clouds**, or "thunderheads" are usually accompanied by severe conditions, including heavy rain and lightning.

Observation	Prediction
Sun and clear sky in the morning	Onshore winds during the day, and offshore winds (land breezes) during the night usually dying in the morning.
Thermal sea breeze	Increasing strength during the day as the land heats up and decreasing or dying at night as the land cools. Expect the wind to veer clockwise as velocity increases. In some parts of the country, increasing sea breezes will be accompanied by growing cumulus clouds.
Calm, overcast days	Continued calm and overcast, unless the sun comes out.
Cold and warm fronts	Showers or rain, changing air temperature, winds shifting in a clockwise direction. Cold fronts usually move faster than warm fronts.
High cirrus clouds	A warm front with rain and changing winds should appear in a couple of days. Clouds will get lower and more dense as the front gets closer.
Cumulus clouds growing taller (cumulonimbus)	Thunderstorms and strong winds.
Dark clouds approaching	A squall or storm

Local Weather Conditions

Weather constantly changes. Recognizing the patterns of your local conditions, such as winds that increase every afternoon, makes planning easier. Some other clues about impending weather are changes in wind direction, cloud patterns and falling temperatures.

The barometer measures air pressure and helps predict weather. A rising barometer usually means good weather approaching, and a falling one warns of poor weather.

A VHF radio tuned to a weather channel keeps you informed about changes and emergencies.

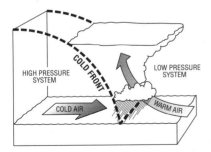

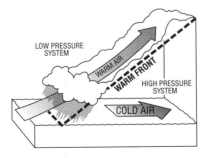

High pressure systems contain cool, dry air that sinks to the ground. When these systems meet warmer air masses, clouds, rain and strong winds can occur. The border where warm and cold masses meet is called a front.

Low pressure systems contain relatively warm air that has a tendency to rise. They move more slowly than high pressure systems and the rain and wind created when they meet cold air masses is less violent.

Getting Ready

It's time to go sailing! Before leaving the dock, however, you need to make your final preparations. The comforts and conveniences of a cruising boat require regular inspections and maintenance. Checking everything over before hoisting sail is a good habit to develop. You also need to familiarize yourself with the wind and water conditions that you might encounter.

Boarding

Step aboard your boat where it's closest to the dock, which is usually in the middle. Place your seabag on board first or have someone hand it to you after you're aboard. Use both hands to grab something solid, like the shroud, and step on the boat's rail before swinging your leg over the lifeline.

SAFETY CHECK

▶ Safety gear

Locate the PFDs, safety harnesses and other safety gear on the boat and make sure you know how to use them. Safety equipment should be stowed so it can be reached easily. Overboard recovery gear, such as a life ring, should be accessible and ready for use.

▶ Engine and other operating systems

It's a good idea to have checklists for the boat's operating systems, especially those which involve through-hull fittings and electricity, such as the engine, head, batteries and electronics. One or two assigned crew members can run through these lists to make sure the boat's ready to go.

▶ Rigging and hull

Check the bilge for water. Familiarize yourself with the rigging. Any potential problems, such as frayed lines or crossed halyards, can be corrected before you leave the dock.

Checking the Sailing Environment

Become attuned to the sailing environment. Many natural and man-made aids can be used to give you information regarding the wind and sea conditions you can expect as you set sail.

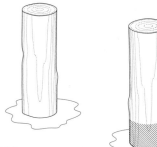

Tides

A dry piling (left) indicates that the tide is rising. A wet piling (right) means that the water level is dropping and the tide falling.

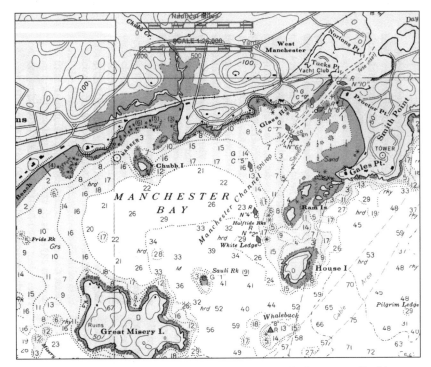

A nautical chart provides many helpful details. Familiarize yourself with a chart of the area in which you're going to be sailing before you leave the dock. Pay attention to navigable channels, buoys, lighthouses, and characteristics of the bottom and soundings. Be sure to note hazards you want to avoid, such as shoals, rocks and other underwater obstructions.

You can "read" the surface of the water. Wind creates waves, which become bigger and steeper as the wind rises. Here you can see the foam crests (white caps) forming on numerous wave tops, which means the wind is blowing about 11 to 16 knots.

Wind speed (knots)	Sea and sailing conditions
0-10	Smooth water with small waves. The boat will be easy to handle under full sail.
11-16	Moderate seas with some white caps. If the boat feels overpowered, consider reefing one of the sails for a more comfortable ride.
17-21	Lengthening waves with many white caps and some spray. Boat will become more difficult to manage and you should seriously consider reefing.
22-27	Large waves, many white caps and spray. Boat will need at least one reef in the mainsail and a smaller jib. These conditions require considerable sailing experience. Listen to radio weather reports for small craft advisories.
28-47	Gale conditions. High waves with white caps and foaming waves. This is a good time to stay ashore!

Rigging the Sails

Think of rigging the sails as getting your boat dressed to go sailing. Start by removing the cover on the mainsail and preparing the lines you'll need to hoist and control the sail. Depending on the wind strength, you'll also make a selection for the proper jib. Use your larger jib for lighter winds and a smaller one for medium and heavy winds.

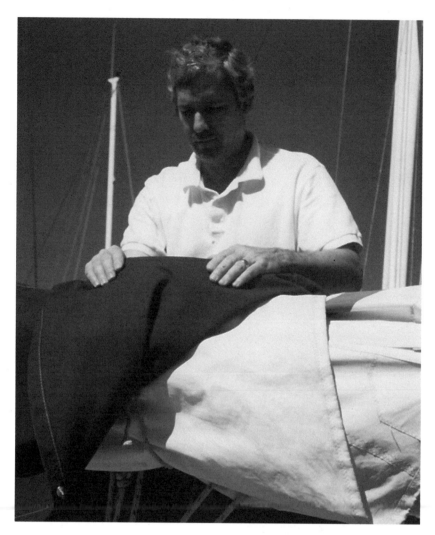

Undo the ties and/or clips that hold the mainsail cover snugly to the boom and mast. Fold or roll the cover up neatly and stow it in a cockpit locker or in the cabin.

Check that the battens are in the mainsail, the reefing lines are adjusted or cleared, and the outhaul is tensioned.

The main halyard fastens to the top of the sail (*head*) in a special reinforced hole. Make sure the halyard shackle is closed securely so the mainsail won't fall down once it's raised.

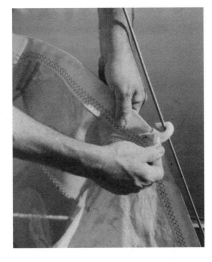

Choosing a Headsail

The smaller (*working*) jib fills the triangle made by the mast, jibstay and deck and is good for medium to heavy winds.

The forward corner (*tack*) of the jib attaches at the base of the jibstay. Again, be sure the connection is secure so the sail doesn't come free unexpectedly.

Attach the front edge of the jib (*luff*) by clipping the special hooks (*jib hanks*) onto the jibstay.

A larger (*genoa*) jib overlaps the mast and gives the boat more power in light to medium winds.

The forward end of each jib sheet ties into the back corner (*clew*) of the jib with a bowline knot, which is both strong and easy to release.

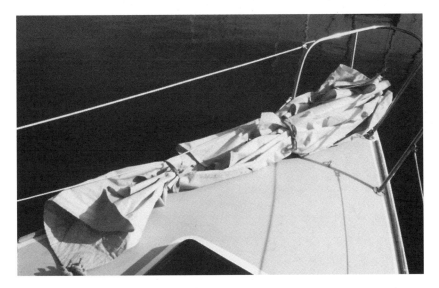

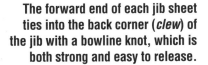

Use a couple of long pieces of webbing (*sail ties*) to wrap the jib into a bundle. Loop the sail ties around a stanchion as well and the sail will lie safely on the deck until you're ready to hoist the halyard. (Don't forget to remove the sail ties first!)

Some jibs are stowed by rolling them around the headstay. You unfurl the sail by pulling the jib sheet and you furl it by pulling on a line attached to a drum at the base of the headstay.

Working as a Crew

A sailing crew is a team and you'll enjoy yourselves more if you learn to work together. Like any team, members need to communicate with one another and know their responsibilities. It may take time to work some of these elements out, but you'll be rewarded with a well-sailed boat and a happy crew!

Big Boat Differences

▶Bigger boats accelerate and turn more slowly than small keelboats. They also glide for more distance, which is important if you're trying to land at a dock.

▶The loads on sheets and halyards are greater on big boats and require caution when handling.

▶Because you're higher off the water, it may not seem like you're going very fast. The increased windage of a larger boat also makes it more susceptible to being blown off course.

▶Repairs on a big boat can be very expensive, so be careful!

Helmsman Responsibilities

The helmsman steers the boat using either the tiller or wheel and tells the crew when the boat is about to tack or jibe. The helmsman reads the compass and determines the boat's course, as well as keeps an eye out for nearby traffic and other obstructions.

COMMUNICATION TIPS

▶ Pay attention to your surroundings and let each other know about possible danger situations.

▶ Talk through maneuvers with other members of the crew before you perform them. Make sure everyone on board knows what's going to happen in advance.

▶ Use hand signals in situations where it's hard to hear or when you're facing forward to perform a maneuver, such as lowering an anchor off the bow.

Mainsheet Trimmer

The mainsheet trimmer trims the mainsheet, adjusts the traveler and keeps an eye out for other boats or obstructions that the helmsman may not see.

Jib Trimmers

The jib trimmers trim the jib and take care of the front part of the boat. They also relay information to the helmsman about oncoming traffic or changing winds.

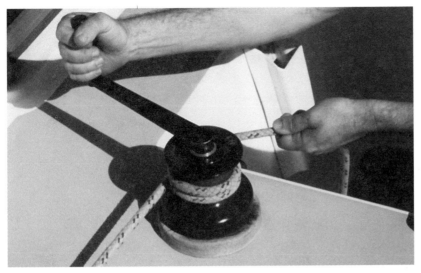

Wrap the line clockwise around the winch one or two times and pull back perpendicular to the axis of the drum. For heavier loads, increase the number of wraps for more friction.

Using a Winch

Used properly, winches can be a sailor's best friend. These revolving drums help you pull halyards and trim sheets. The friction of the line on the drum reduces the strain on your hands. At the same time, the pressure on the winch can be very great, so don't get anything caught between the line and the drum such as jewelry, clothing, hair or other body parts!

Release the line by pulling the wraps up and off the drum.

For better leverage, stand or stoop over the winch, grab the winch handle with two hands and use your upper body to grind.

To ease a line, hold the tail in one hand and push against the wraps on the winch with the palm of your other hand. Release the line slowly, a couple of inches at a time.

Winch wraps are a hazard. Don't get your fingers caught in one!

Dealing with an Override

Sometimes a line will wrap on a winch and jam. Don't panic! You can free a winch in one of several ways.

▶ **If the load is light,** simply unwrap the line counterclockwise.

▶ **If the line is firmly jammed,** use another line led to another winch to take the load off. Then unwrap the original line.

▶ **If you can't unload the line easily,** take the loose tail of the jammed line to another winch, wrap it clockwise and grind the line free.

Leaving the Dock

Marinas differ and you will need to know how to leave from a side dock as well as a slip. Discuss how you plan to leave the dock and what each person will do. Before you start the engine or undo lines, check the wind velocity and direction, and the current.

Key Points

▶ Be sure everyone knows what to do.
▶ Check that no lines are in the water before starting the engine.
▶ Get on and off the boat at the shrouds.
▶ Stow the docklines and fenders after you clear the dock.

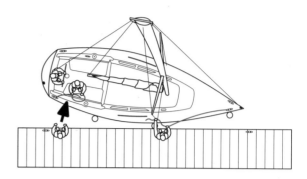

Stern departure

❶ A crew member uncleats the stern line, then pushes the stern out and boards the boat at the shrouds, while a second crew member holds onto a shroud and the bow line.

Bow departure

❶ The docklines have been released and a crew member stands on the dock holding onto the boat with the stern line in hand.

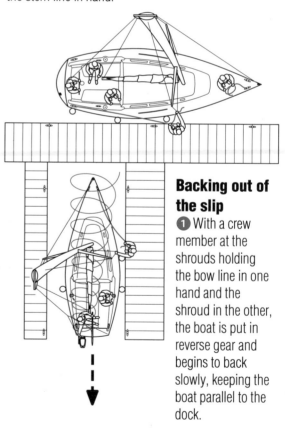

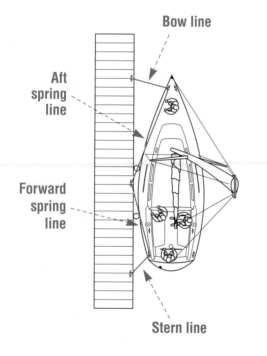

Bow line

Aft spring line

Forward spring line

Stern line

Note: Aft and forward spring lines do not refer to their position on the boat, but the direction in which they restrain or pull on the boat.

Backing out of the slip

❶ With a crew member at the shrouds holding the bow line in one hand and the shroud in the other, the boat is put in reverse gear and begins to back slowly, keeping the boat parallel to the dock.

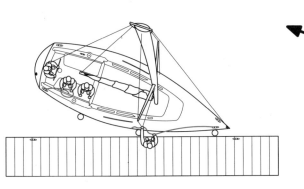

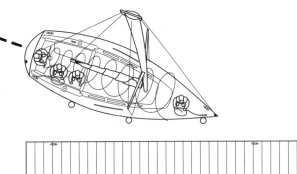

❷ The second crew member makes sure the stern is cocked away from the dock before boarding at the shrouds.

❸ In reverse gear, the boat is backed away from the dock while crew members coil lines and stow fenders.

❷ The crew member then pushes off and steps aboard at the shrouds with stern line in hand.

❸ In forward gear, the boat is steered away from the dock in a gentle turn so the stern won't hit the dock, while crew members coil lines and stow fenders.

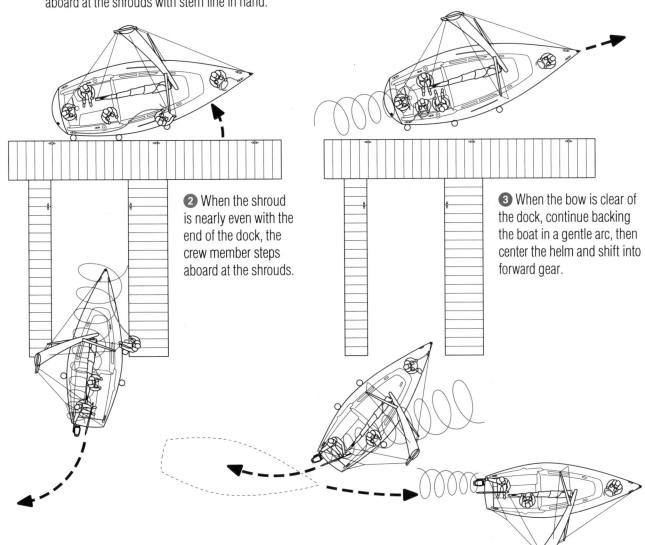

❷ When the shroud is nearly even with the end of the dock, the crew member steps aboard at the shrouds.

❸ When the bow is clear of the dock, continue backing the boat in a gentle arc, then center the helm and shift into forward gear.

Steering

Sailboats are steered with either a tiller or a wheel, which is connected to the rudder. The rudder turns the boat by directing the water flow. A sharp turn of the rudder slows your forward motion. If you turn the rudder too far, the water flow will stall and your helm (*tiller or wheel*) will feel unresponsive. Regardless of the steering system, you have to be moving through the water in order for the rudder to turn the boat.

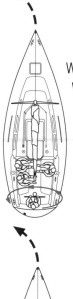

With a **steering wheel**, turn the wheel in the direction you want to turn just as you would a car.

With a **tiller**, move it opposite to the direction you want to go.

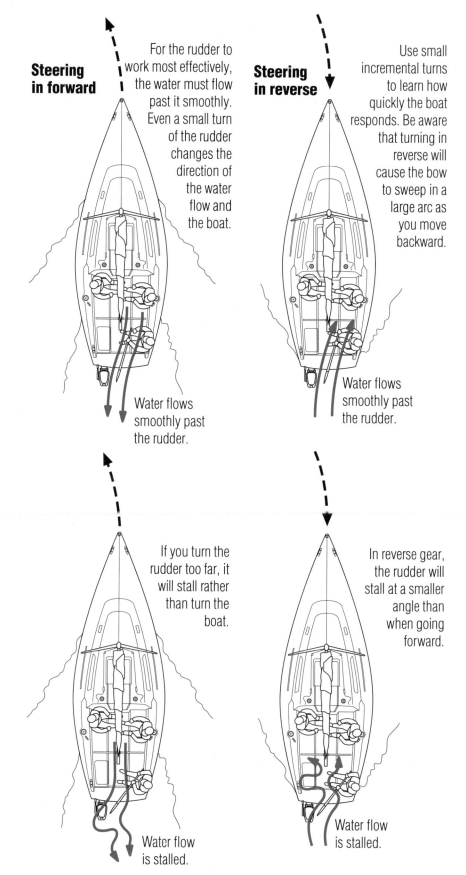

Steering in forward

For the rudder to work most effectively, the water must flow past it smoothly. Even a small turn of the rudder changes the direction of the water flow and the boat.

Water flows smoothly past the rudder.

If you turn the rudder too far, it will stall rather than turn the boat.

Water flow is stalled.

Steering in reverse

Use small incremental turns to learn how quickly the boat responds. Be aware that turning in reverse will cause the bow to sweep in a large arc as you move backward.

Water flows smoothly past the rudder.

In reverse gear, the rudder will stall at a smaller angle than when going forward.

Water flow is stalled.

Windage

Under power, a boat responds to the wind as it pushes on the hull. The effect of this push (*windage*) can change the way the boat moves, and will vary with the amount and direction of the wind. With practice, you'll learn to compensate for windage.

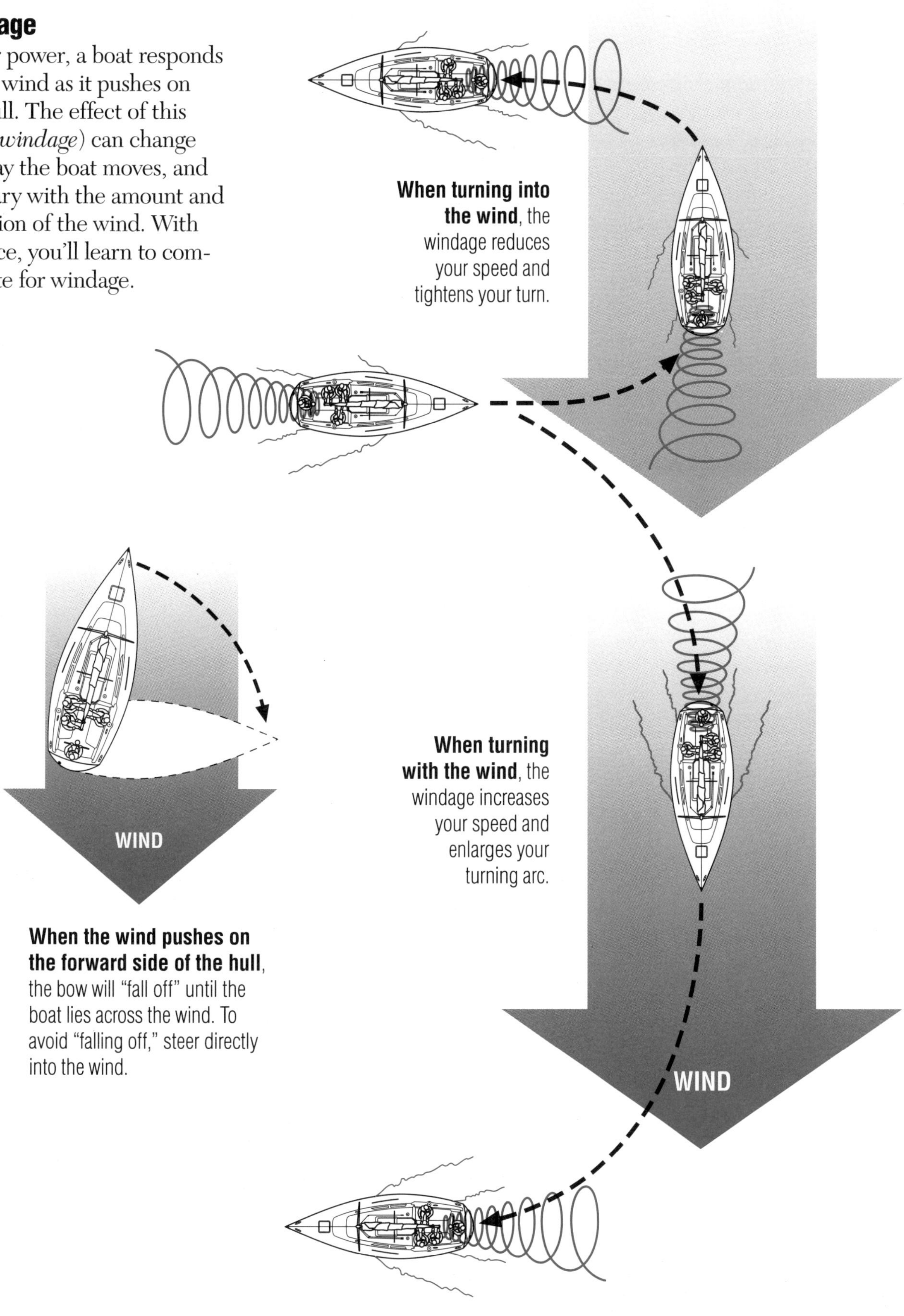

When turning into the wind, the windage reduces your speed and tightens your turn.

When turning with the wind, the windage increases your speed and enlarges your turning arc.

WIND

When the wind pushes on the forward side of the hull, the bow will "fall off" until the boat lies across the wind. To avoid "falling off," steer directly into the wind.

WIND

Stopping

Stopping the boat under power is an important step in learning to dock. Always check your reverse gear to make sure it's working. When stopping into the wind, the pressure of the wind on the hull and rig (*windage*) will help slow you down. When stopping with the wind, windage will push the boat, so you may need to increase the reverse throttle and allow more distance to come to a standstill.

Bigger boats and heavier boats have more forward momentum and coast farther than small boats. The bigger the boat, the more distance you'll coast.

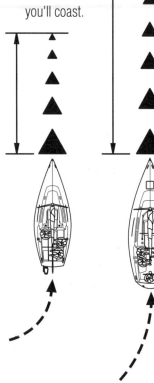

You can stop without using reverse, but you need to allow more distance to coast.

Using reverse gear permits you to stop in much less distance. Always slow the engine and pause briefly before shifting to reverse gear. Then increase reverse power until the boat stops at the desired spot.

Prop Walk

Prop walk is the tendency of your boat to turn slightly rather than go in a straight line. The cause is the propeller's direction of rotation. This tendency can be put to good use when you understand which way it moves your boat. You can test your "prop walk" direction by putting the boat in reverse while you are parallel to the dock, and see if the stern swings toward or away from the dock.

Using Prop Walk

Dock the boat on the side that it "walks" to. Approach the dock slowly in a gentle arc. As you reach the dock, reverse your engine and let the stern "walk" over to the dock.

The propeller in reverse "walks" the stern to port.

Slight turn to port.

The boat with the larger arc has used only the tiller to turn.

The boat with the smaller arc has turned both the tiller and the outboard motor in the same direction.

Using the Outboard Prop

If you have an outboard motor, you can use it to help turn your boat. With both the rudder and motor turned in the same direction, you will be able to make a much tighter turn than if you just turned the rudder. Compare the arcs of the two boats.

Hoisting the Main

When you've found an open space of water with no nearby obstructions, you can hoist your mainsail. Leave the engine in idle in case you need power before the sails start working. Turn the boat directly into the wind so the sail luffs as it's being hoisted. Leave the running rigging (*mainsheet, cunningham, outhaul, reefing lines and boom vang*) loose until the sail is fully raised and the halyard cleated. Then adjust the sail controls and pull in the sail.

Before attaching the halyard to the top corner of the mainsail (*head*), look up to make sure the line isn't wrapped around anything.

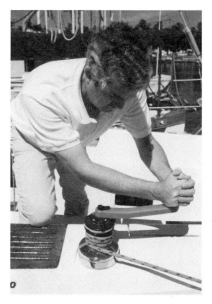

Raise the sail smoothly. If the halyard sticks, stop and correct the problem before proceeding.

Raise the mainsail first with the jib ready to hoist.

After securing the main halyard, coil the end of the line neatly so it can run freely if you need to lower the sail quickly.

Attach the coiled halyard to the cleat where you can reach it easily.

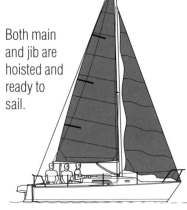

Both main and jib are hoisted and ready to sail.

Hoisting the Jib

After the mainsail is up and ready, you can continue heading into the wind or turn slightly to one side so the wind partially fills the sail. Leave the jib sheets loose as you hoist. After securing the halyard, trim the sail.

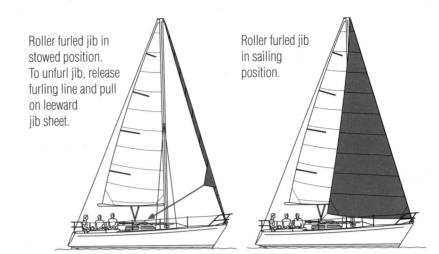

Roller furled jib in stowed position. To unfurl jib, release furling line and pull on leeward jib sheet.

Roller furled jib in sailing position.

Do's and Don'ts

▶ Don't grind the halyard up if you meet resistance. Do keep an eye aloft to make sure the sail or halyard isn't stuck or wrapped around anything. Also, make sure you stop when the sail is fully hoisted.

▶ Don't stand too close to the boom as the sail is raised. The luffing sail will shake the boom, sometimes vigorously.

▶ Don't get in the way of hoisting the jib. Do stand clear of the sail and the sheets as the sail goes up and starts to luff.

▶ Don't turn off the engine until your sails are up and working. At that point, if the auxiliary is a diesel, stop the engine before you turn off the ignition key.

If the front part of the jib shows vertical wrinkles (*below left*), the halyard is too tight. Ease the halyard just enough so that the wrinkles disappear and the front of the sail is smooth (*below right*).

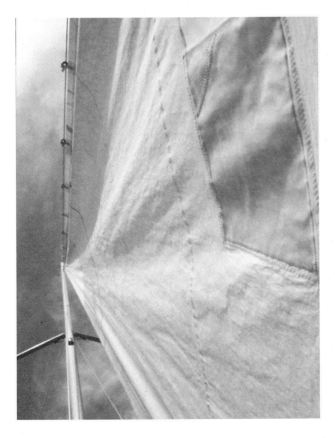

Sailing Upwind

Sailing upwind requires some practice. The sail must be trimmed in all-the-way and the boat must be steered attentively. After awhile, you'll find "the groove" where the boat is progressing toward the wind (*to windward*) and moving easily through the water with a comfortable amount of heel (*sideways tipping*). Well-trimmed boats will have a slight tendency to head up toward the wind (*weather helm*).

The sails are trimmed all-the-way in so that the wind flows smoothly off both the main and jib.

STEERING TIPS

▶ Don't oversteer the boat. Make your course changes small ones for a smoother ride.

▶ Use the masthead fly and telltales to help sail "in the groove."

▶ Head up slightly in puffs to keep the boat from heeling over too much.

▶ Keep your head up to watch the sails and the wind on the water as it approaches you.

On a steering wheel, a piece of tape or line gives you a reference point (the **king spoke**) for when the rudder is centered. With a slight weather helm, this mark will be positioned slightly off center.

The deck level wind direction readout (**apparent wind indicator**) gives you the angle of the wind relative to the boat's centerline.

The **masthead fly** points to the direction from which the wind is blowing. With practice, you'll sense how close you can steer to the wind and stay in the groove.

Working Together

Coordination between the helmsman and crew will help sail the boat upwind faster and more efficiently. Communicate with each other about sail trim and changes in the wind strength and direction.

Jib Trimmers

Trim the jib and let the helmsman know when puffs of wind are coming. Also look out for other boats or obstructions.

Mainsheet Trimmer

Trims the mainsheet. If the boat heels too much, the trimmer eases the mainsheet to get the boat back to a comfortable angle of heel.

Helmsman

Steers a "snake" course upwind, sailing as close to the wind as possible to gain distance to windward and then away from the wind a little to maintain speed. Calls for in and out adjustments in sail trim.

When the windward telltale (on the side closest to the wind) flutters and the jib luffs, the helmsman needs to steer away from the wind (*head down*) until the telltale stops fluttering.

On a well-trimmed jib, both of the telltales on the front edge of the sail are streaming back.

Sailing Downwind

After sailing upwind, turning downwind (*"easing sheets"*) is more relaxing and comfortable. The sails must still be trimmed properly relative to the wind direction, but the motion of the boat is usually more gentle. Don't become too relaxed, however! You must still keep an eye out for other boats. If the wind shifts or you sail too far away from the wind, the boat could jibe accidentally, throwing the boom across the cockpit suddenly.

By the Lee

When the wind comes from behind the mainsail (*sailing by the lee*), the boom can swing across the cockpit out of control. If the jib goes limp and starts to cross the boat, this is a warning that you're sailing by the lee. You can prevent an accidental jibe by heading back up toward the wind. If not, be sure everyone ducks his or her head as the boom comes across.

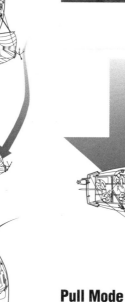

Pull Mode
Sailing across the wind or upwind, the wind flowing along both sides of a sail creates higher pressure on one side than the other side, which pulls the boat forward.

Push Mode
On a broad reach and a run, the wind simply pushes against the sails and moves the boat forward.

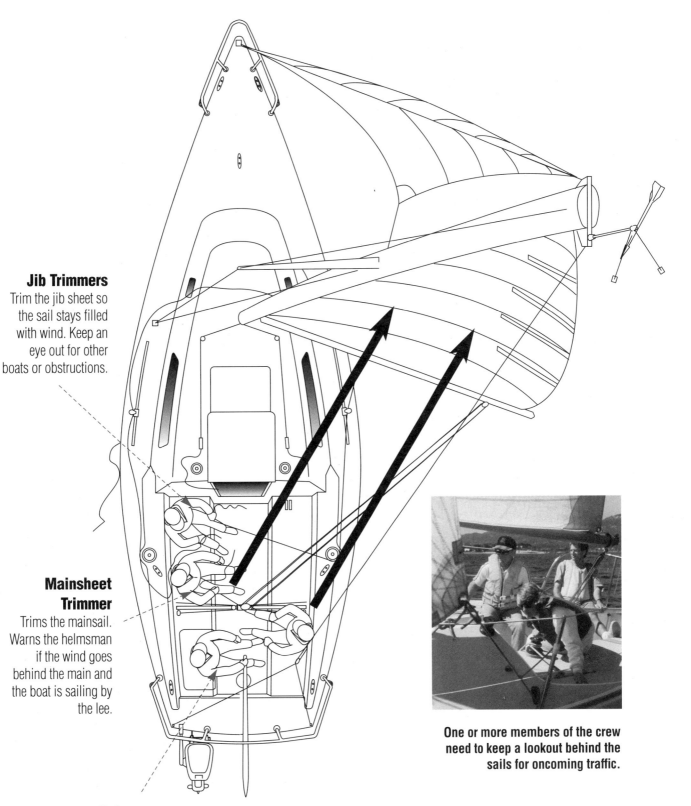

Jib Trimmers
Trim the jib sheet so the sail stays filled with wind. Keep an eye out for other boats or obstructions.

Mainsheet Trimmer
Trims the mainsail. Warns the helmsman if the wind goes behind the main and the boat is sailing by the lee.

Helmsman
Steers the boat in a straight course, watches for oncoming traffic and monitors the masthead fly to prevent the boat from sailing by the lee.

One or more members of the crew need to keep a lookout behind the sails for oncoming traffic.

Tacking

Steering the bow of the boat from one side of the No-Go Zone to the other is called tacking. During the tack, the sails cross from one side of the boat to the other. The crew trimming the jib releases the sheet so the sail can pass in front of the mast. The new jib sheet is then pulled in all-the-way so the boat can sail upwind again.

④ Helmsman resumes sailing upwind. Crew coils sheets in preparation for another tack.

WIND

WIND

③ Helmsman completes the tack after reaching the edge of the No-Go Zone. Crew pulls in the sheet until the jib stops luffing.

The boat is ready to tack. One of the jib trimmers prepares to release the sheet holding the jib while the other prepares to pull in the opposite sheet after the jib passes in front of the mast.

"Tacking!" or *"Hard a-lee!"*

"Ready!"

"Ready about!"

② Helmsman announces the tack and turns the boat into the No-Go Zone. Crew releases the working sheet and makes sure the line runs free.

① Helmsman gives the command that the boat is about to tack. Crew position themselves at the jib sheets before responding, *"Ready!"*

"Ready!"

"Jibing!" or "Jibe-ho!"

1 Helmsman gives the command that the boat is about to jibe. Crew position themselves at the jib sheets and get ready to pull in the mainsail before responding, "*Ready!*"

Jibing

The opposite of tacking, jibing turns the stern of the boat through the wind. During a jibe, you should control the boom by sheeting it in before the boat crosses the wind and letting the sheet out quickly afterward. To jibe the jib, simply release the sheet. Let the sail pass in front of the mast and resheet it again on the other side of the boat.

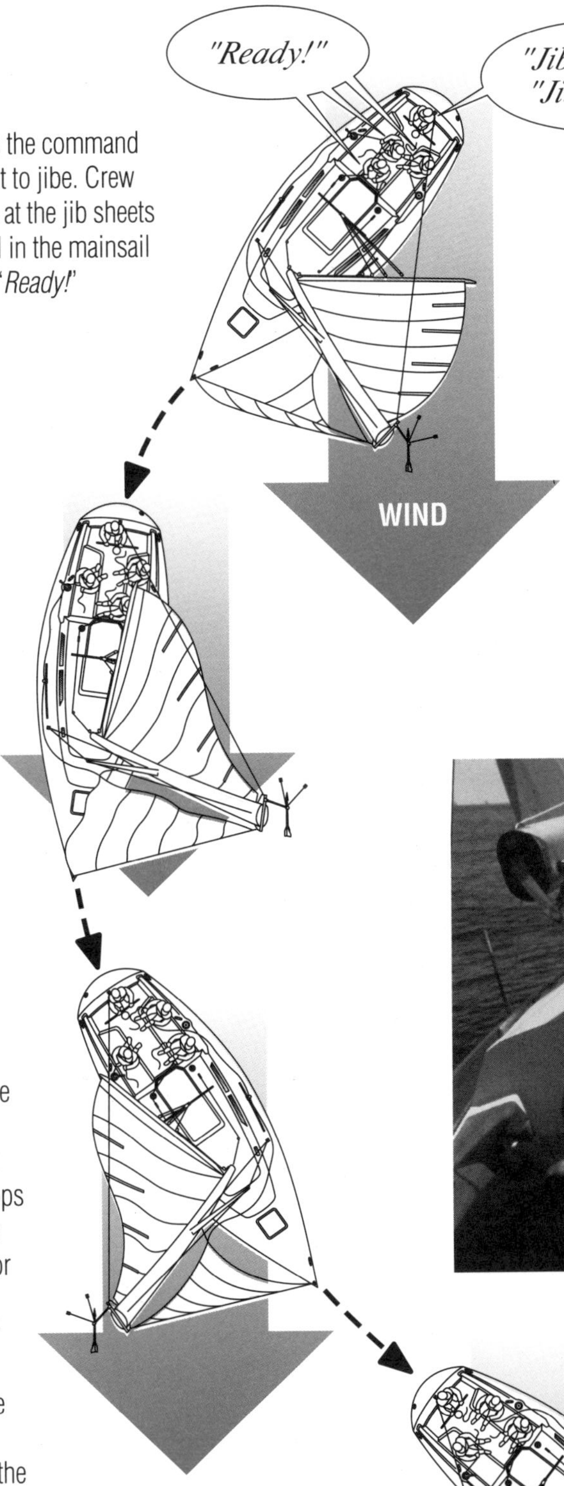

2 Helmsman turns the boat away from the wind. A crew member pulls the mainsail to the center of the boat. Jib sheet is released so the sail can cross over.

WIND

3 Helmsman continues to turn the boat as the boom comes across. Just before the boom flops over, the helmsman calls out "*Jibing!*" or "*Jibe-ho!*" as a warning. Keep your head down! Crew member lets out the mainsheet so the boom can assume the proper sailing angle.

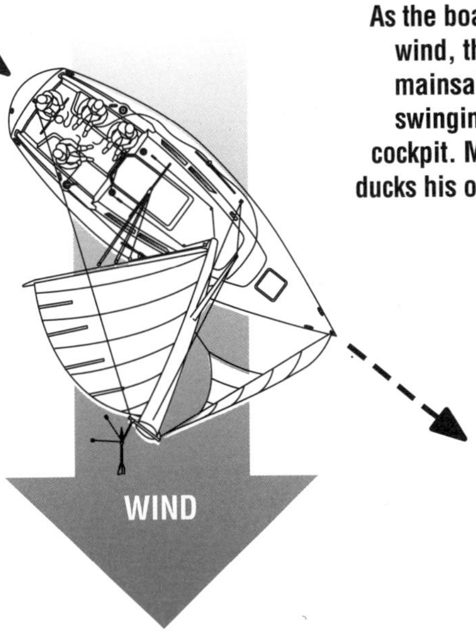

As the boat turns through the wind, the crew pulls in the mainsail to prevent it from swinging wildly across the cockpit. Make sure everyone ducks his or her head during a jibe!

4 Helmsman puts the boat on the new course. Mainsail and jib are trimmed to the proper setting.

WIND

Lowering Sails

Give yourself plenty of room to maneuver as you lower the sails. Make sure that the crew is ready and no lines are trailing in the water that might get caught in the propeller. To slow the boat, turn into the No-Go Zone and let the sails luff. Then start the engine and let it idle in neutral or use it to keep the boat into the wind.

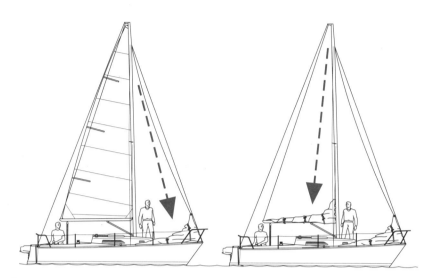

Lower the jib first and secure it to one side with sail ties to the rail or stanchions. Before lowering the mainsail make sure the toppinglift is in place to support the boom and the traveler is centered and secured. Then lower the sail and fold it, making it fast to the boom.

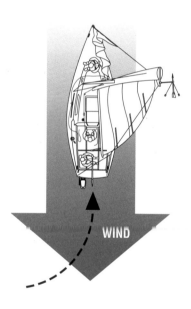

WIND

Many sailors turn the boat into the wind, the No-Go Zone, to lower the sails. Another technique is to turn downwind and lower the jib behind the mainsail. Secure the jib on the deck and turn the boat back into the wind to lower the main.

With the toppinglift ❶ supporting the boom, the mainsail is folded on top of the boom and secured with sail ties.

With fenders in place, and bow and stern lines coiled, these crew members are ready to step off at the shrouds when the boat comes alongside the dock.

Crosswind Docking - leeward side

When the wind is blowing away from the dock, the boat's windage will push you away from the dock. **1** Turn the boat into the wind. **2** About half a boat length from the dock, make a tight turn to bring the boat parallel to the dock. **3** Reverse the engine to stop. Secure bow and stern lines quickly and then secure the spring lines.

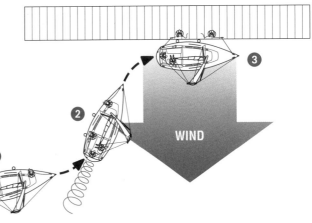

Crosswind Docking - windward side

When the wind is blowing onto the dock, the boat's windage will push you onto the dock. **1** Approach the dock at an angle. **2** Turn the boat parallel to the dock about half a boat length away from the dock. **3** Reverse the engine to stop the boat, and use the boat's windage to drift to the dock. Secure the stern line and then the other lines.

Downwind Docking

Docking with the wind requires more distance to stop the boat because windage is pushing the boat forward. **1** Approach the dock at a 45 degree angle. **2** Make a gradual arc putting the engine in neutral. **3** As you reach the dock, put the engine in reverse and open the throttle briefly to stop the boat. Use the stern line to counteract the windage. Make the bow line fast and then secure the other lines.

Upwind Docking

It's easier to dock into the wind because windage helps to stop the boat. **1** Approach the dock at a 45 degree angle. **2** Make a smooth turn into the wind. **3** Reverse the engine, stopping the boat alongside the dock. Secure the stern line to prevent the boat from drifting backward and then secure the other lines.

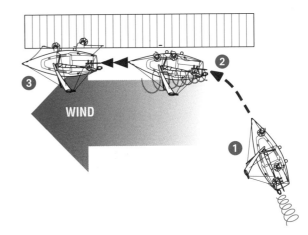

Returning to the Slip

Bringing the boat into a slip uses many of the
same techniques as the previous page. However,
you have to judge your stop more precisely to
avoid hitting your bow on the dock.

Upwind Slip

1 Make a wide easy turn toward the slip.
2 Put the engine into neutral and let the
windage slow the boat, then reverse the
engine to stop the boat in the slip. **3** Crew
members step onto the dock and secure the
bow and stern lines.

WIND

Downwind Slip

1 Turn the boat toward the slip.
2 Reverse the engine to stop the
boat. **3** Let the windage push the boat
into the slip, reversing the engine as
needed to control the speed and bring
the boat alongside the dock. Crew
members step onto the dock using the
bow and stern lines to help stop the
boat and then make them fast.

WIND

Crosswind Slip

1 Turn the boat so that it is parallel to
and upwind of the slip. **2** Reverse the
engine to slow the boat. **3** Let the
windage and momentum glide the boat
into the slip, and reverse the engine to
stop the boat. Crew members secure
the docklines.

WIND

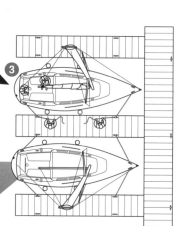

Securing the Boat

The boat can be tied along the side of a slip using single bow and stern lines and spring lines, or it can be secured with two bow lines and two stern lines.

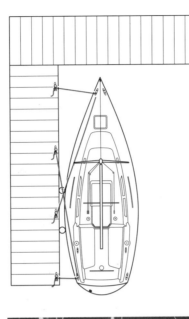

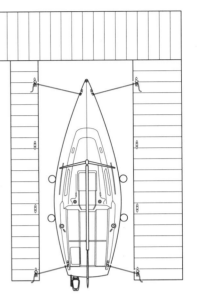

CHECKLIST

► Close seacocks.
► Remove trash and take perishables ashore.
► Turn off all electrical switches and the main battery switch.
► Cover sails or stow them securely.
► Stow winch handles, blocks and lines.
► Plug in shore power.
► Tidy and clean deck.
► Lock companionway.
► Inspect all docklines.
► Check fender placement.

The mainsail will last longer if you use a **sail cover** to protect the sail and reefing lines from ultraviolet rays.

The individual switches and the battery switch should be in the **OFF position**. Check to make sure the automatic bilge pump is on after turning off the battery switch.

Before leaving the boat, make sure the **hatch boards** are in place, and the sliding hatch is secured with a lock.

Don't forget to plug in the **shore power** to keep your battery charged.

Adjusting Sail Shape

You can adjust the shape of the sail for different wind conditions. A sail with more curvature (*fuller*) from front to back gives you more power in light winds. A sail with less curvature (*flatter*) performs better as the wind builds and you want to depower to keep the boat under control and sailing well.

A fuller sail has more power for light winds.

A flatter sail works better in high winds.

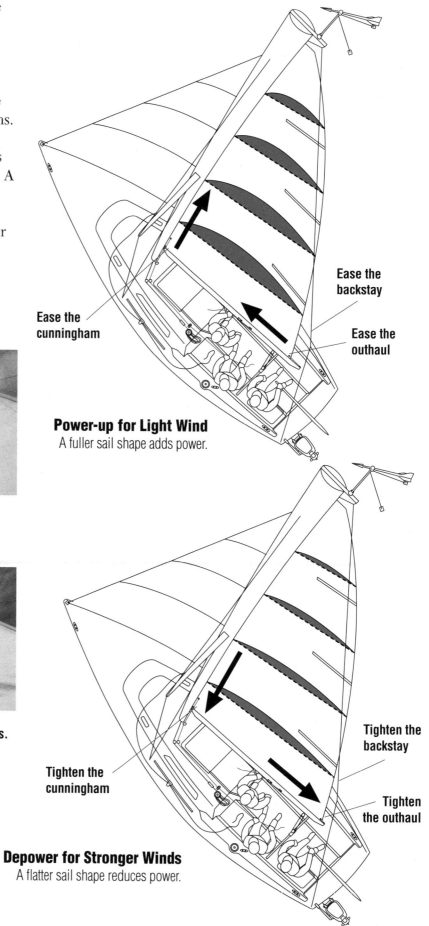

Ease the cunningham

Ease the backstay

Ease the outhaul

Power-up for Light Wind
A fuller sail shape adds power.

Tighten the cunningham

Tighten the backstay

Tighten the outhaul

Depower for Stronger Winds
A flatter sail shape reduces power.

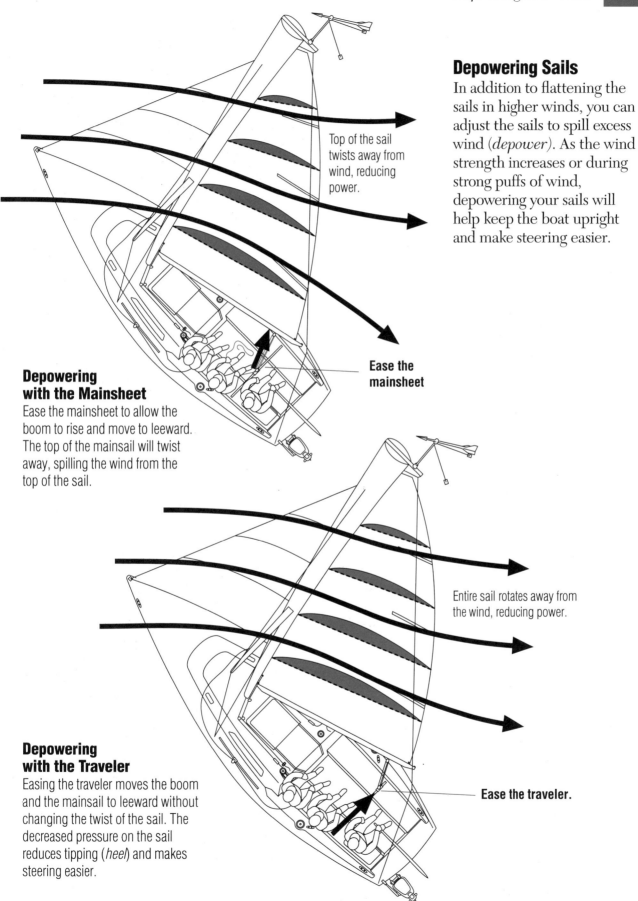

Top of the sail twists away from wind, reducing power.

Ease the mainsheet

Entire sail rotates away from the wind, reducing power.

Ease the traveler.

Depowering Sails

In addition to flattening the sails in higher winds, you can adjust the sails to spill excess wind (*depower*). As the wind strength increases or during strong puffs of wind, depowering your sails will help keep the boat upright and make steering easier.

Depowering with the Mainsheet

Ease the mainsheet to allow the boom to rise and move to leeward. The top of the mainsail will twist away, spilling the wind from the top of the sail.

Depowering with the Traveler

Easing the traveler moves the boom and the mainsail to leeward without changing the twist of the sail. The decreased pressure on the sail reduces tipping (*heel*) and makes steering easier.

Shortening Sail

Shortening sail is another way to keep your boat in balance and under control when the wind increases. You can choose several options for reducing sail, depending on what's available on your boat, the wind and sea conditions and the direction from which the wind is blowing. Remember, the best time to shorten sail is before your boat becomes overpowered!

Heeling the boat over and fighting the pull on the helm may feel powerful, but the force of the extra wind only pushes the boat sideways and creates drag on the rudder. You'll sail safer and faster with the boat more upright and the helm more balanced.

A simple way to shorten sail is to change down to a smaller jib, which will reduce the sideways force on the sails and help keep the boat upright.

Most boats have a system for reefing the mainsail by lowering the sail and tying the lower portion to the boom.

When sailing in very strong winds, you can sail with main alone, which will tend to turn the boat into the wind (*weather helm*) when a puff hits.

Leaving the working jib up reduces sail area. Reaching in heavy seas, the jib will also resist the boat's tendency to turn into the wind (*round up*) when the boat rolls. Make sure the mast is adequately supported.

Changing Headsails

Changing headsails, especially in high winds, requires planning. Work with other crew members to get the job done. The wind will want to catch a loose sail on the deck, so make sure you have control of the new jib before it's hoisted and the old jib after it's lowered.

1 Bring the folded sail to the headstay and attach the tack to the bow fitting. Then connect the luff to the headstay, starting with the bottom hanks. You may have to remove the first few fasteners of the raised jib to do this.

2 Unfold the new sail. Lower the raised jib and secure it with sail ties or remove it from the deck. Connect the sheets to the new jib.

3 Attach the jib halyard to the new jib and make sure it's clear to hoist.

4 Hoist the new jib completely and then trim the sail.

Roller Furling

Some boats have roller furling jibs, which are attached to a rotating rod on the forestay. The main advantage of this system is that you can furl and unfurl the jib without having to go to the foredeck. In high winds and large seas, this can be an important safety factor.

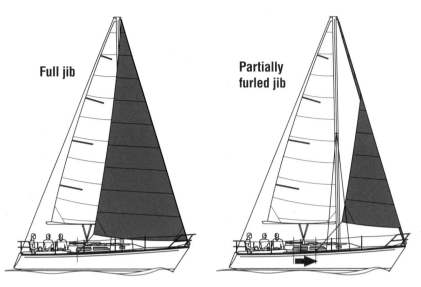

Full jib

Partially furled jib

To furl the jib, uncleat the jib sheet so the sail can luff. Pull the furling line until the sail wraps itself around the headstay and then cleat the line so the sail won't come loose unexpectedly. To unfurl the sail, uncleat the furling line and pull on the leeward jib sheet.

Roller furling drum

Furling line

The furling line is led aft along the side of the boat to a cleat in or near the cockpit. From here, you can control the size of the jib without going forward.

If you furl the jib part way and continue sailing (don't forget to cleat the furling line so the sail won't unroll!), you'll need to move the fitting for the jib sheet (*jib fairlead*) forward. This will maintain a proper trim angle for your jib sheet.

Do's & Don'ts

▶ Don't try to furl a trimmed jib. The load on the sail will make the job too hard and you may damage the roller furling equipment.

▶ Don't rely on a partially furled jib for extremely long periods of time. The sail may not be made for heavy weather reefing.

Slab Reefing

Most boats are set up to reef by lowering the mainsail and tying off the lower section (*slab reefing*). The procedure is relatively quick and easy (which is why it's also called "jiffy" reefing). Like changing jibs, reefing the main requires that you follow a standard procedure.

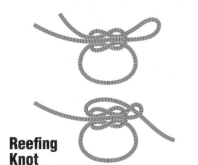

After the sail has been secured at both ends of the boom, tie the loose part in the middle to the boom with short pieces of line led through holes in the sail (*reefing eyes*).

Reefing Knot

Tie a square knot with a loop and pass the other end of the line back through the loop. Then take the slack out of the loop to secure the knot.

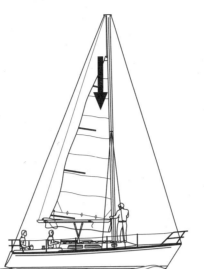

1 Loosen the mainsheet and boom vang. Support the end of the boom by tensioning the toppinglift. Lower the main halyard until the large reinforced hole on the front of the sail (*luff cringle*) can be passed over the hook or horn at the front end of the boom.

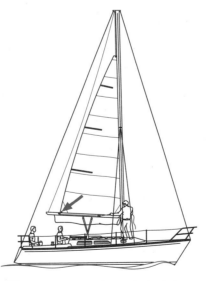

3 When the leech cringle is tight on the boom, secure the reefing line. Ease the toppinglift, trim the mainsheet and readjust the boom vang. Lead a safety line through the leech cringle and tie it around the boom.

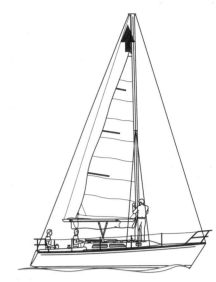

2 Retighten and secure the halyard. Start to haul in the reefing line to bring the hole at back edge of the sail (*leech cringle*) down to the boom.

Do's & Don'ts

▶ When reefing in rough conditions, be careful of the swinging boom! If you have to go forward to the mast, wear a PFD or attach your harness to the boat with a tether.

▶ Make sure your mainsail luffs fully while you lower the halyard and pull in the reefing line. Keep the jib trimmed so the boat continues moving forward.

▶ Use reference marks on the main halyard to know how far to drop the sail when reefing.

▶ To remove the reef, reverse the order of events that you used to shorten sail.

Types of Anchors

Anchors hold a boat in position where there are no docks or other places to tie up near shore. Anchors vary in size, shape, weight and materials according to where they're being used and to the preference of the sailors using them. You attach the anchor to your boat by rope or chain, or a combination of both.

Lightweight-type Anchor

A lightweight-type anchor, such as a Danforth, has two large flukes that bury into the bottom. The anchor is light and easy to handle and stow.

Plow-type Anchor

As its name implies, the plow-type anchor digs into the bottom and holds well. This is a good all around anchor, although it is heavier than the lightweight-type.

Bruce Anchor

The Bruce anchor has a large, spoon-like blade that buries itself quickly, which makes it especially useful in crowded anchorages.

Anchor type	Works well in...
Lightweight	sand, hard mud, soft clay bottoms
Plow	sand, mud, clay, grass and rocky bottoms
Bruce	sand, mud, clay, grass and rocky bottoms

To set an anchor, get the angle of pull (angle of attack) as close to horizontal as you can. This will help dig the anchor's flukes into the bottom. A more vertical angle of pull will prevent the flukes from burying or break the anchor free.

Setting An Anchor

Since you usually can't see your anchor once it goes overboard, you need to know how it works. Anchors dig into the bottom and hold best when pulled from a low angle. Let out plenty of line to help set the anchor. You'll feel a solid pull when it buries itself.

Scope

Scope is the ratio of the length of your anchor line (*rode*) **1** to the depth of the water **2** Adequate scope varies from 4:1 to 7:1 depending on various factors such as the amount of chain in your rode (less scope) or rough weather (more scope).

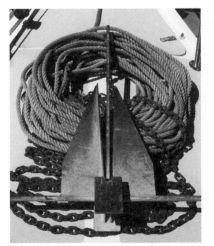

A length of chain between the anchor and the nylon rode helps weigh down the line, which gives you a better angle of attack to set the anchor.

Extra protection on the anchor line where it comes on board protects against chafe.

Anchoring Decisions

You need to weigh several factors when you're looking for a suitable place to anchor. Some of the information, such as depth of the water, type of bottom and effects of current, can be gleaned from your nautical charts. Use your powers of observation for other considerations, such as protection from wind and waves and how other boats anchored nearby will react to changes in wind and current.

Anchoring factor	Solution
Depth of water	Water deep enough so boat can swing in a complete circle around the anchor at low tide. Not so deep that you won't have enough anchor line.
Bottom type	Sandy bottoms are always good. Avoid long thick grass and soft mud, as well as underwater cables and moorings.
Protection	Anchor downwind (in the lee) of land or a breakwater and be prepared for a wind shift. Don't anchor near boat traffic.
Room to swing	Make sure your boat can swing a complete circle without hitting anything, such as a dock, breakwater or other boats.
Current	Take into account the direction and strength of the current, which may change while you're anchored.

Anchoring with other boats

Your anchor becomes the center of a circle about which your boat can rotate. Knowing how much anchor line and chain you have out tells you how big that circle will be. Changes in wind or current will cause your boat to swing, so try to anchor near similar types of boats and you'll all swing together.

Boats with deep underbodies sometimes react more to the current than to wind direction while anchored.

Boats with lots of windage react more to wind direction while anchored.

Reactions to Wind and Current

Different types of boats swing differently at anchor. Powerboats and multihulls sit on top of the water and respond more to the wind. Sailboats with low freeboard and deep keels are more sensitive to the water passing underneath the surface, especially in light winds.

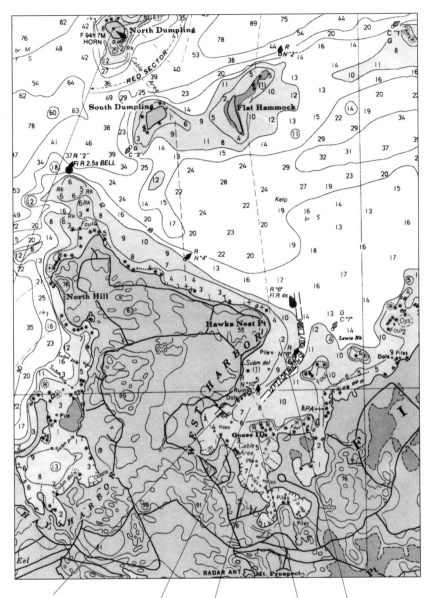

These docks might be a place to find provisions or fuel.

Keep clear of the rocks!

This looks like a good place to anchor: plenty of water and room to swing if the wind or current changes.

Avoid putting down an anchor near cables. Hooking one will ruin your day.

Watch out for the 2-foot shallow area next to the harbor channel. Don't even think of anchoring here!

Preparing to Anchor

Before you actually lower the anchor overboard, prepare the boat and the crew. Bring the anchor up on deck and make sure the connections between the anchor and rode (*chain and line*) are secure. Coil the line so it will run freely. Lead the anchor under the bow pulpit so the anchor line will feed out from the bow through the special fitting (*chock*). Also, consult your chart of the area to find the best spot to anchor.

The crew is ready to lower the anchor, with the rode coiled and the anchor line led under the pulpit.

Anchoring Under Power

While you can anchor under sail, you'll have more control and maneuverability, especially with other boats or obstructions nearby, if you furl sails and use the engine. One or more members of the crew should be at the bow to lower the anchor and send back information to the helmsman.

2 Bring the boat to a stop and lower the anchor over the bow. Make sure everyone stands clear of the rode as it pays out. When the anchor hits bottom, slowly start to back directly downwind or parallel to the boats around you.

1 Approach the anchoring spot slowly. Check the water depth to make sure you won't hit bottom, even if the water level falls with the tide. Prepare to make your final approach either directly upwind or from the direction in which other boats nearby are lying.

3 Let the anchor rode pay out as the boat moves away from the anchor. The bow watcher should indicate (with hand signals if necessary) if the boat needs to be turned to keep the boat going backward in a straight line.

4 When at least five times as much rode has paid out as the depth of water at high tide, wrap the line around a cleat. The momentum of the boat will help set the anchor. Once the boat has stopped moving, pay out more rode to achieve the optimum scope ratio.

This is the hand signal for the helmsman to steer to port.

This is the signal for the helmsman to steer to starboard.

If the helmsman should go straight, raise a hand and motion forward.

When it's time to stop, raise a clenched fist.

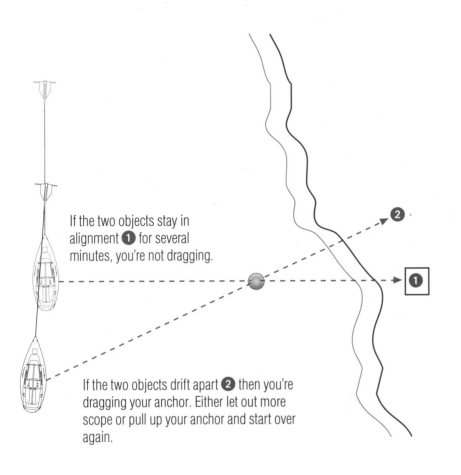

Is Your Anchor Secure?

Once you've lowered the anchor and paid out the rode, how do you know if the anchor's holding? An easy way is to sight two stationary objects, like a tree and a building, that are aligned off the side of your boat. Don't use another anchored boat, however, since it may be swinging and therefore not truly stationary.

If the two objects stay in alignment **1** for several minutes, you're not dragging.

If the two objects drift apart **2** then you're dragging your anchor. Either let out more scope or pull up your anchor and start over again.

Raising an Anchor

To raise anchor and get underway, reverse the procedure you used to anchor. As the rode's angle of attack becomes more vertical, it should pull the anchor free. If not, tie off the rode and use your engine to change the angle of pull or to break the anchor free.

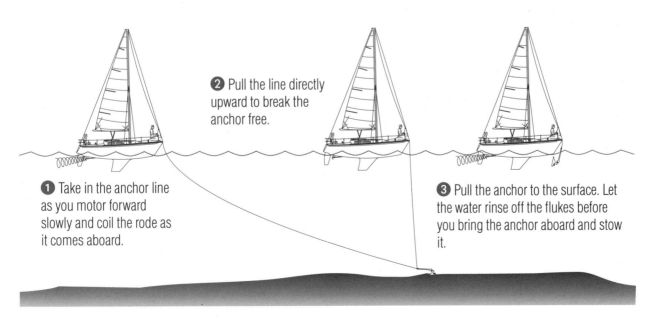

2 Pull the line directly upward to break the anchor free.

1 Take in the anchor line as you motor forward slowly and coil the rode as it comes aboard.

3 Pull the anchor to the surface. Let the water rinse off the flukes before you bring the anchor aboard and stow it.

Using Spring Lines

Muscle power isn't always enough to push the boat from the dock. A spring line works as a lever to turn the boat when you power against it.

Reminders

▶ Be sure crew members know when and how to release the lines.

▶ Always take in the spring line quickly to avoid wrapping it on the propeller.

▶ Retrieve the fenders and stow them and the lines after you clear the dock.

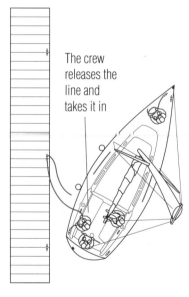

The crew releases the line and takes it in

Doubling a Dockline

Doubling a dockline is a very useful technique that allows you to release the line from aboard the boat as you leave the dock. To double back a line, pass it around the dock cleat and back to the boat.

Springing off with the aft spring line

1 With the aft spring line doubled, cast off the bow and stern lines and then the forward spring line. Center the helm and put the engine into slow forward.

Springing off with the forward spring line

1 With the forward spring line doubled, cast off the bow and stern lines and then the aft spring line. Center the helm and put the engine into reverse gear with slow throttle.

Docking at a pier with pilings

1 Steer the boat straight between the pilings passing close to the windward one so a crew member can put a stern line loop over the top of the piling. The other end of the line should go to the after deck cleat.

Note: Pilings often have rope stops which keep the dockline loops from slipping down them. For pilings without stops, you will need to tie the docklines to the pilings.

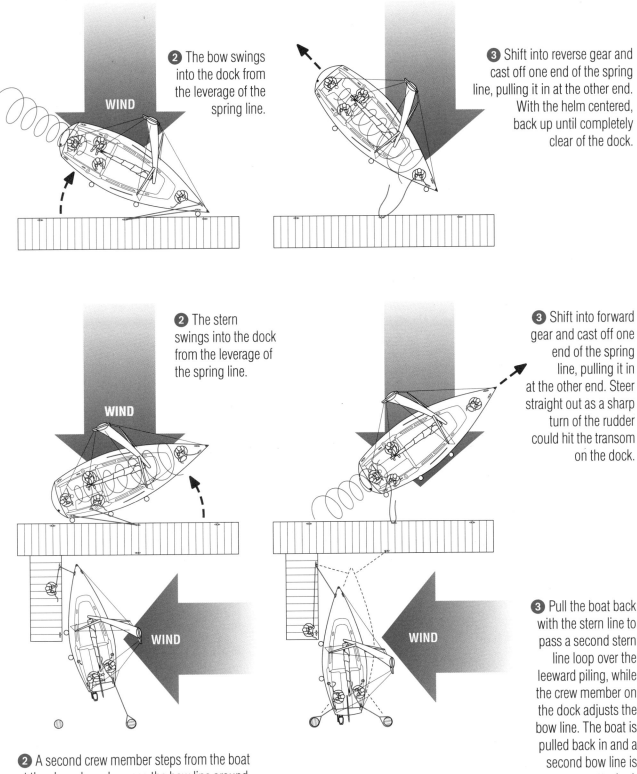

2 The bow swings into the dock from the leverage of the spring line.

WIND

3 Shift into reverse gear and cast off one end of the spring line, pulling it in at the other end. With the helm centered, back up until completely clear of the dock.

2 The stern swings into the dock from the leverage of the spring line.

WIND

3 Shift into forward gear and cast off one end of the spring line, pulling it in at the other end. Steer straight out as a sharp turn of the rudder could hit the transom on the dock.

WIND

WIND

2 A second crew member steps from the boat at the shrouds and passes the bow line around the dock cleat while the first crew member eases out the stern line.

3 Pull the boat back with the stern line to pass a second stern line loop over the leeward piling, while the crew member on the dock adjusts the bow line. The boat is pulled back in and a second bow line is attached.

VHF Radio

A VHF radio provides local marine weather forecasts, communication with nearby boats and marinas, and access to emergency assistance. The VHF radio is capable of line-of-sight transmission. To operate a VHF you must have a Ship's Station License issued by the Federal Communications Commission.

The console mounted VHF radio uses the boat's battery for power and has an installed antenna, which gives it greater range than the hand-held model (below). Adjust the squelch control by turning it down just under the crackling sound.

NOTE: For best results, stand clear of the shrouds and mast, and have a fully charged battery pack. Remember to turn off the power when not in use.

Radio Communication Basics

▶ Use only those channels identified for recreational boating.

▶ Radio waves are public and shared. Speak clearly, be brief and be polite.

▶ Always give way to any vessel calling in an emergency.

▶ When making a call, identify the boat you're calling, then identify yourself, using the boat's name and/or call sign (a call sign is the number assigned by the FCC in the Ship's Station License). EXAMPLE: *"Squeeker, Squeeker, Squeeker, this is Cat's Paw, Whiskey-Oscar-Romeo 6789er. Over."* The call sign is WOR 6789, but the phonetic alphabet is used in radio transmissions.

▶ When ending a call, use "out" instead of "over." EXAMPLE: *"This is Squeeker, Whiskey-Quebec-Romeo 1234. Out."*

▶ When making a *life-threatening* emergency "Mayday" call, remember the three W's: <u>WHO</u> you are, <u>WHERE</u> you are, and <u>WHAT</u> is your type of distress, situation and seaworthiness. When calling, repeat "Mayday" and your boat's name or call sign three times and then repeat. EXAMPLE: *"Mayday, Mayday, Mayday, this is Squeeker, Squeeker, Squeeker. Mayday, Mayday, Mayday, this is Squeeker, Squeeker, Squeeker. We are half a mile north west of Pt. Sur. We have lost our mast and rudder and cannot start engine. I have two severely injured crew. There are three people on board, hull is okay, but no steerage or power. This is Squeeker, Whiskey-Quebec-Romeo 1234. Over."*

▶ If the emergency is not life-threatening, but is urgent, use "Pan, Pan, Pan" instead of "Mayday, Mayday, Mayday." If it's a warning, use "Securite, Securite, Securite."

▶ "Over" indicates that you have ended your transmission and expect a response from the other person.

▶ "Out" indicates that the transmission is ended and no response is expected.

Channel Designations

1,2,3,4 - Weather - Provide continuous local marine weather forecasts, including storm warnings and watches.

09 - Used for communication with other vessels, marinas and port captains. Also, an alternative hailing channel in areas where channel 16 is congested. It is NOT an emergency channel.

13 - Bridge to Bridge Communication - Reserved for communication between commercial vessels.

16 - EMERGENCY/Hailing - Used for emergency calls or calling other vessels and land bases. Upon receiving a response, advise the other boat to switch to a non-commercial vessel channel.

68,69,71 - Non-Commercial Vessels - Used for communication with other boats, marinas and port captains. Switch to one of these channels after hailing on 16.

72 - Non-Commercial Intership - Used solely for communication with other vessels. Switch to this channel after hailing on 16. There are also local designations for bridge, lock, river and lake navigation. The Coast Guard may have special channels in your area.

Stoves

Stoves on cruising boats are generally available in several sizes and types. Two-burner alcohol stoves are common on smaller boats while larger boats may have gimballed, propane gas stoves with ovens. Some stoves may have compressed natural gas (CNG) for fuel, but they are limited to use in the U.S.

Stove Operation

Propane gas is efficient and inexpensive but must be used with care. To operate the stove, open the valve at the tank and open the solenoid switch to bring the fuel to the stove. When finished cooking, turn off all burners and the solenoid switch. Always close the valve at the tank when you leave the boat.

Alcohol stoves require preheating of the burners to vaporize the fuel. When the burner is hot, the fuel can be turned on and ignited for cooking. Because alcohol is a cool flame, it cooks slowly and is easily extinguished. Keep a pan of water handy to put out an alcohol fire.

Small cruising boats often have alcohol stoves which have a cool flame and don't take up much space.

The stove is usually gimballed to stay level regardless of heel.

Do's & Don'ts

▶ Always turn off any cooking fuel when the stove is not in use.
▶ Ignite the match or starter before turning on the propane burner.
▶ Never overfill the preheat rim of an alcohol stove.
▶ The stove should be in the gimballed position when underway, and locked when at the dock.

Propane tanks have a shutoff valve which should be closed when the stove is not in use for a period of time.

A solenoid switch is located near the stove to turn the propane on and off. Be sure to turn it off when you have finished cooking.

Knots

Part of the sailor's skill is using knots to secure lines. These knots also need to come untied easily so the line can be moved or reused. You only need to learn a handful of knots, however, in order to handle most situations. Practice tying and untying these knots so they'll be second nature when you need them in a real situation.

Cleating a Line

Wrap the line around the base of the cleat and then cross it over the top.

Loop the line around one horn of the cleat and then twist the line to form a loop around the other horn.

The end of the line should parallel the part of the line that was originally crossed over the top of the cleat.

Bowline

The bowline (BOE-lin) puts a non-slipping loop at the end of a line. The knot becomes more secure under pressure, but remains easy to untie. It is the most commonly used knot on sailboats. Among its many applications, the bowline is used to attach the jib sheets to the clew of the jib.

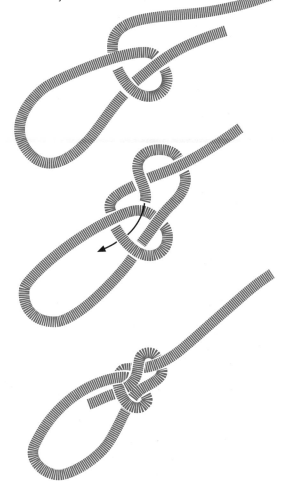

To tie a bowline, put a small loop in the line where you want the knot to be, for example, about 18 inches from the end. Make sure the end crosses on top of the standing part of the line. This small loop will end up as part of the knot.

Run the end up through the loop you just made, down behind the standing part, back up over the edge of the loop, and down through the loop again.

Snug the knot together, making sure the knot holds and the remaining loop does not slip.

Figure-8 Knot

The figure-8 knot looks like its name. It is sometimes called a stopper knot, and is tied on the end of a line to keep the line from slipping through a fitting. Easy to untie, it is commonly used on the ends of the jib sheets in the cockpit.

Pass the end over the standing part.

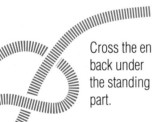

Cross the end back under the standing part.

Bring the end down through the loop. Tighten the knot.

Square Knot

The square knot is used only for sail lashings. It is not recommended for tying two lines together because it can be difficult to untie.

Tie a simple overhand knot with the right end going over the left.

Tie another simple overhand knot, this time crossing left end over right end.

As you tighten the line the knot should be symmetrical.

Sheet Bend

A sheet bend is used to tie two different size lines together. It looks like a bowline, and it is secure and easy to untie.

Make a loop at the end of the larger line, with the bitter end crossing over on top. Run the smaller line up through the loop.

Run the smaller line down around the standing part of the larger line, up over the edge of the loop, and down through the loop again.

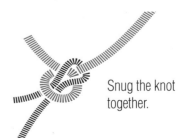

Snug the knot together.

Rolling Hitch

The rolling hitch holds a line to a solid object, like the mast, or takes the strain of another line without slipping. You can tie an extra line to the jib sheet with a rolling hitch, for example, when you need to change the fairlead but don't want to release the sail.

Clove Hitch

A clove hitch is used to tie a line to an object. It is not a very secure knot. It is very easily untied and, with an extra half-hitch, is commonly used to tie fenders onto lifelines.

Two Half-hitches

This knot should use a loop to secure a line to an object.

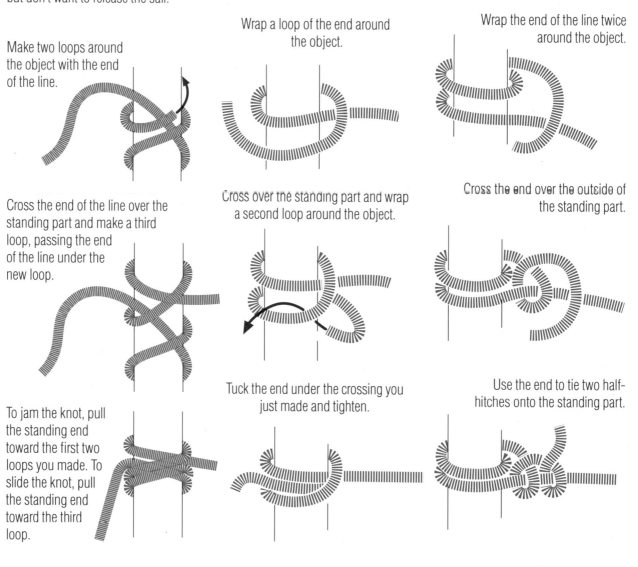

Make two loops around the object with the end of the line.

Wrap a loop of the end around the object.

Wrap the end of the line twice around the object.

Cross the end of the line over the standing part and make a third loop, passing the end of the line under the new loop.

Cross over the standing part and wrap a second loop around the object.

Cross the end over the outside of the standing part.

To jam the knot, pull the standing end toward the first two loops you made. To slide the knot, pull the standing end toward the third loop.

Tuck the end under the crossing you just made and tighten.

Use the end to tie two half-hitches onto the standing part.

Coiling a Line

A line should not be simply left in a tangled pile, but should always be ready to use or release by leaving it coiled.

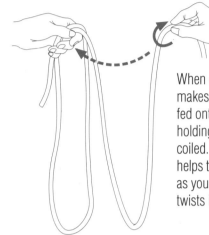

When coiling a line, one hand makes a new loop which is fed onto the other hand holding the loops previously coiled. With some lines, it helps to twist the line slightly as you coil to avoid kinks or twists in the line.

To stow a coiled line, wrap the end of the line around the middle of the coil. Make a loop and pass it over one end of the coil, pulling the end of the line to secure it.

Heaving a Line

When preparing to throw a line, make sure one end is secured on your boat. Hold half of the coil in your throwing hand and the other half in your other hand. Swing and throw the coil underhand, allowing the remainder of the line to run free from your other hand.

Tides and Currents

Tides are the *vertical* movement of water and are caused primarily by the gravitational pull of the moon on the earth. As the moon rotates around the earth, it "pulls" the earth's water toward it. As the moon moves, so does the water level in most bodies of ocean water. Typically there are two high and two low tides each day on the east and west coasts of the U.S. In the Gulf of Mexico there is usually only one high and one low per day. With a watch, a tide table and a chart you can determine the depth of the water in which you are sailing or anchoring at any given time.

A current is the *horizontal* movement of water and is caused by a river's flow, wind, and ocean movements. The Gulf Stream off the East Coast of the U.S. is a well known ocean current. In coastal areas, currents are also caused by the tides going out (*ebb*) and coming in (*flood*) to bays along the coastline. Depending on their direction, these currents can either assist or hinder your progress while sailing. It is important to know the direction and strength of currents. Charts, tide tables, and a watch are helpful in planning your sail.

These photos, taken at the same location, show the difference between high and low tide. Consulting a tide table and a chart will help you avoid running aground during a low tide.

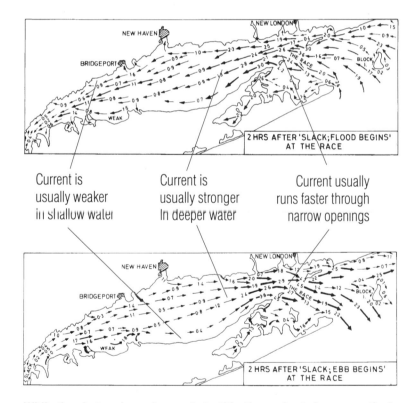

Current is usually weaker in shallow water

Current is usually stronger in deeper water

Current usually runs faster through narrow openings

While the photos above demonstrate *tide*, these charts from a nautical almanac show *current* caused by tides coming in (*flooding*) and going out (*ebbing*) of Long Island Sound. Charts courtesy Reed's Nautical Almanac

Reading Tides and Current

There are a number of indicators on the water and shoreline that will tell you what the tide and currents are doing.

Current

This buoy is being pulled by the current. You can see that it is leaning in the direction of the current, and the moving water is leaving a wake as it passes the buoy.

A tide table gives you daily information regarding the exact times of high and low tides and the heights of the tides.

NEWPORT, RI
HIGH & LOW WATER — 41°30'N 71°20'W
CORRECTED FOR DAYLIGHT SAVING TIME: APRIL 2 – OCTOBER 28

RHODE ISLAND

Table courtesy Reed's Nautical Almanac

Compensating for Current

If you are going to sail across a current you can compensate for the effect it will have on your boat. Instead of steering directly toward your goal, steer for a point upstream, and let the current pull you back to your desired course.

035°

020°

CURRENT

This boat aimed directly for its destination (035 degrees) but was pulled downstream by the current.

This boat steered a course (020 degrees) upstream of its goal and reached its planned destination.

Navigation Rules Under Sail

The basic purpose of the Navigation Rules is to avoid collisions. The boat that has right-of-way is the stand-on vessel and should maintain course and speed. The give-way vessel must keep out of the way and should make its change of course obvious and early. It is always a vessel's obligation to avoid collisions even if it has the right-of-way.

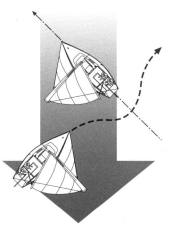

◄ Starboard Tack over Port Tack

When sailboats approach on opposite tacks, the boat on starboard tack has the right-of-way and is the stand-on vessel. The port tack boat, or give-way vessel, should change course to pass behind the other boat.

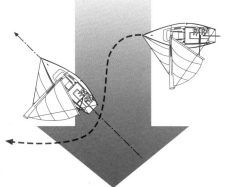

Leeward over Windward ▶

When two sailboats meet on the same tack, the upwind *(windward)* boat is the give-way vessel and should steer behind the leeward boat, which is the stand-on vessel.

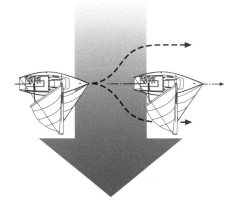

Overtaken over Overtaking ▲

The boat that is doing the passing is the give-way vessel and may pass to either side of the stand-on vessel. The stand-on vessel should hold its course.

Commercial Vessels over Pleasure Craft ▲

Ships in channels, tugboats with tows and working commercial fishing vessels are stand-on vessels and have the right-of-way over sailboats.

Sailboats over Powerboats ▲

When sailboats and powerboats meet, the sailboat is the stand-on vessel. The powerboat is the give-way vessel because it is more maneuverable.

Navigation Rules Under Power

When your sailboat is propelled by an engine, you are a powerboat. Even when motorsailing, you must comply with the rules for power. Sound signals are exchanged to communicate intended course changes. The long blast is four to six seconds in duration while the short blast is just one second. Five or more short blasts is the danger signal. When you hear this signal it means a dangerous situation exists or your intended course change is not acceptable. Boats under 12 meters in length (about 39 feet) are not required to carry sound devices, but you're smart to be prepared.

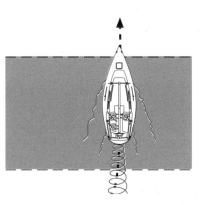

▲ Traffic separation zones or vessel traffic lanes are reserved for use by large vesels and others with restricted maneuverability. You should stay clear of these zones. If it's necessary to cross a zone, do it at a 90 degree angle (or as close as you can) and as quickly as possible.

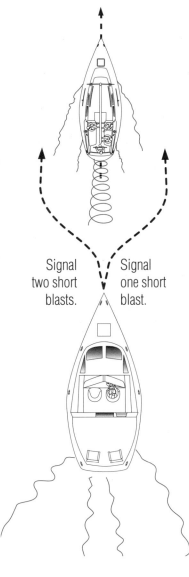

Signal two short blasts.

Signal one short blast.

◄ Overtaking

The passing (*overtaking*) boat is the give-way vessel and may pass to either side of the stand-on vessel.

Note: When overtaking on international waters, the signal is two long blasts and one short blast when altering course to starboard and two long and two short when altering course to port. Acknowledgment is responding with the same signal.

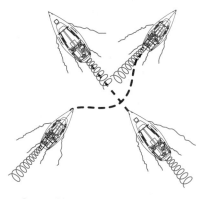

▲ Crossing

When two boats are on an intersecting course, the boat on your starboard side is the stand-on vessel, and you must alter course as the give-way vessel.

Head-on ▼

When two boats approach each other, they should alter course to starboard to pass port side to port side and signal accordingly. (*If you alter to port and pass starboard side to starboard side, the signal and response is two short blasts.*)

Acknowledge with one short blast to show agreement.

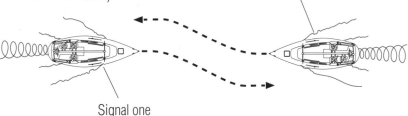

Signal one short blast.

Basic Navigation Aids

Buoys and channel markers are like road signs and traffic markers on the water. While there are many kinds of buoys and channel markers in use in North America, the most common ones fall into the categories shown here. They have distinct shapes and colors that will help you sail your boat in and out of harbors safely and avoid shallow water. The basic rule to remember in U.S. waters is *"Red, Right, Returning."* This means keep the red markers to your right when you are returning from open water into a harbor. Red channel markers are usually paired with green ones. Keep the green buoys on your right when leaving a harbor into open water.

A **green daymark** is a square, odd-numbered green sign that is mounted to a piling. It marks the side of a channel and should be treated like a can.

A **red daymark** is a triangular, even-numbered, red sign mounted to a piling. It marks the right side of a channel when returning.

Green or red **lighted buoys** are usually spaced relatively far apart and located near the entrances of harbors. Each has a distinct flashing pattern that is indicated on a chart so it can be readily identified. Lighted buoys are especially helpful for navigating at night.

A **can** is an odd-numbered, green buoy that is used to mark the *left* side of a channel when entering (or returning to) a harbor. It has a flat top. When you leave a harbor, cans mark the *right* side of the channel.

A **nun** is an even-numbered, red buoy used to mark the *right* side of a channel when entering (or returning to) a harbor. It has a pointed top. When you leave a harbor, nuns mark the *left* side of the channel.

Green and red striped **junction buoys** mark channel junctions and obstructions. You can pass on either side, but the preferred side is indicated by the color of the topmost band.

Reading a Chart

A chart shows not only the channels and the buoys, but also the shorelines, the water depth, obstructions, shoals, the positions of wrecks, and characteristics of the bottom. In addition, it indicates the positions of landmarks, lighthouses and much more. At the edge of the chart is an important note: "Soundings in Feet," "Soundings in Meters," or "Soundings in Fathoms" which tell you how the water depth is measured on the chart. A meter is a little over three feet, while a fathom is precisely six feet. Always check which distance is used to indicate water depths (*soundings*) on your chart.

Charts indicate **onshore landmarks** that can be used as navigation references. Here a tower is indicated.

These diamond shapes are **channel markers**. On a chart they are colored to represent a nun (*red*) or can (*green*). In this channel you can see a set of cans (*on the left*) and nuns (*on the right*) positioned to guide you safely through the narrow channel opening.

A **contour line** follows a constant water depth. On most charts, areas of shallower waters are indicated by a light blue area.

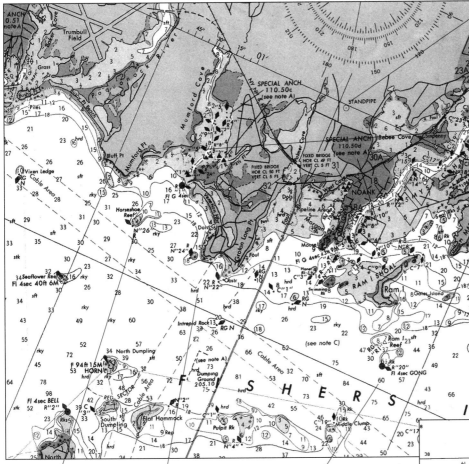

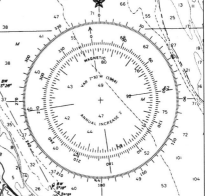

Charts also indicate noteworthy bottom topography, such as hazardous rocks, sunken ships, reefs (shown) and other **hidden dangers**.

Charts indicate the **type of bottom**, such as hard, rocky, sand, or mud that you can expect when looking for a place to anchor.

The small numbers scattered throughout the water are **soundings** or depths at low tide at those particular points.

A **compass rose** (right) is printed on every nautical chart.

Planning with Chart and Compass

With a compass and chart you can determine your location when you're sailing. These same tools can be used to plan where you want to go. For instance, you are at point **A** on the chart and want to sail to point **B** and then return to point **C**, West Harbor. Draw a line from **A** to **B**, and then draw a line from **B** to **C**. Make sure there are no hazards such as rocks, reefs and shallow waters along the route.

Now, transfer the lines from A to B and B to C to the compass rose. The lines have been drawn for you. Read the circled heading at the letter "B" on the compass rose. The heading is 272 degrees, which is your compass course from A to B. At B you will change course to sail to letter C, West Harbor. The circled heading drawn on the compass rose for letter "C" indicates a compass course of 196 degrees.

To sail the course you have planned, just steer to the compass headings you have plotted.

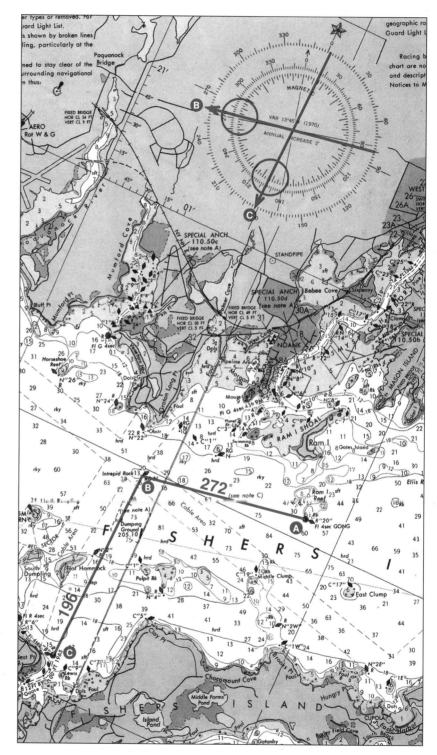

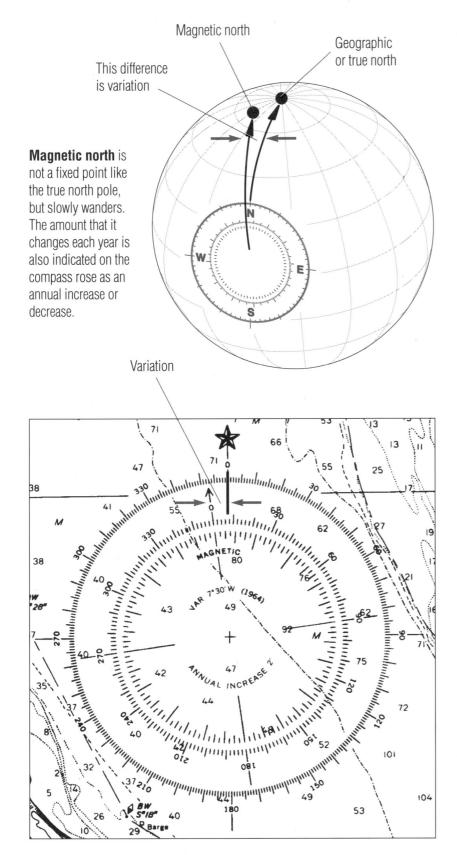

Magnetic north

This difference is variation

Geographic or true north

Magnetic north is not a fixed point like the true north pole, but slowly wanders. The amount that it changes each year is also indicated on the compass rose as an annual increase or decrease.

Variation

Compass Variation

Your compass points to magnetic north, but your charts are oriented to true north. The difference in degrees between your compass readings and true north is called variation. The amount and direction of variation will vary depending on your location. The compass rose on your chart will indicate the amount and direction of the variation for your sailing area.

Magnetic items on the boat can affect the magnetic readings of the compass. These magnetic differences are called deviations.

Compass Deviation

Your compass responds to iron or steel objects which have magnetic properties. The difference in compass readings created by their magnetic influence is called the deviation. For instance, a bag of tools accidently placed next to the compass can cause a deviation so that the compass reads 75 degrees when it really is 80 degrees.

Plotting

Plotting, marking locations and courses on a chart, helps you record your progress or plan your trip. Plotting tools, like course protractors and parallel rulers, are used to transfer the course direction information on the chart to the compass rose, and vice versa. With the distance scale on the chart and the dividers, you can measure how far you've progressed or plan how far you want to go.

Plotting a course with parallel rulers requires "walking" the rulers in parallel across the chart to transfer information to or from the compass rose.

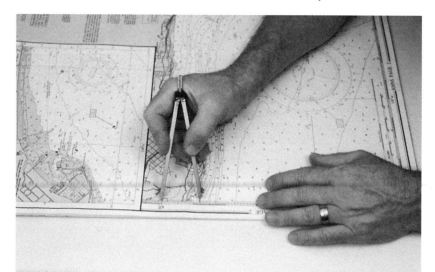

Use dividers to match the chart scale (*above*) to distances on the chart (*right*) and vice versa.

The course protractor is a tool used to mark the course you have sailed or determine the course you want to sail.

Determining Your Position

You can use the bearings (*directions*) to fixed objects from your boat to determine your position and plot it on the chart. In the example below, the bearings from three objects have been transferred to the chart and their intersection (called a *fix*) indicates the boat's position. In actual practice, rarely do all three lines pass through the same point, but they will form a small triangle. Your position is usually inside the triangle.

The hand bearing compass (*right*) is more accurate for taking bearings because you can position the object just above the numbers on the compass.

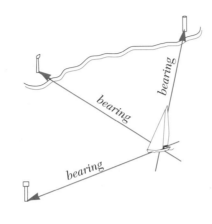

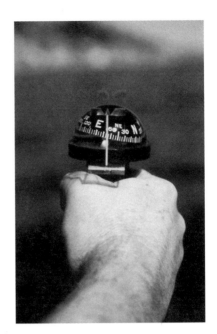

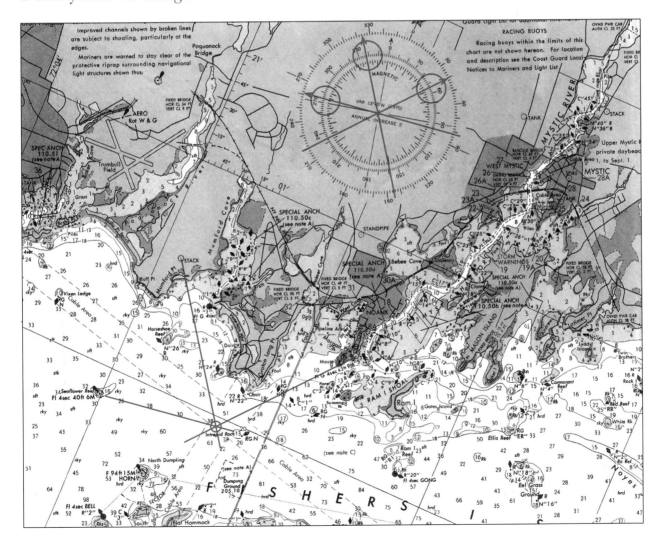

Time, Speed and Distance

Speed at sea is measured in knots, which are nautical miles per hour. By understanding the relationship between time, speed and distance, you can estimate how long it will take to reach a destination or use it to determine your location.

The relationsip between time, speed and distance can be remembered by using this simple formula:

Speed (**S**) = $\frac{\mathbf{D} \text{ (miles)}}{\mathbf{T} \text{ (hour)}}$ or **S** = $\frac{60^* \times \mathbf{D} \text{ (miles)}}{\mathbf{T} \text{ (minutes)}}$

*60 converts hours to minutes

Calculating Speed

In the example 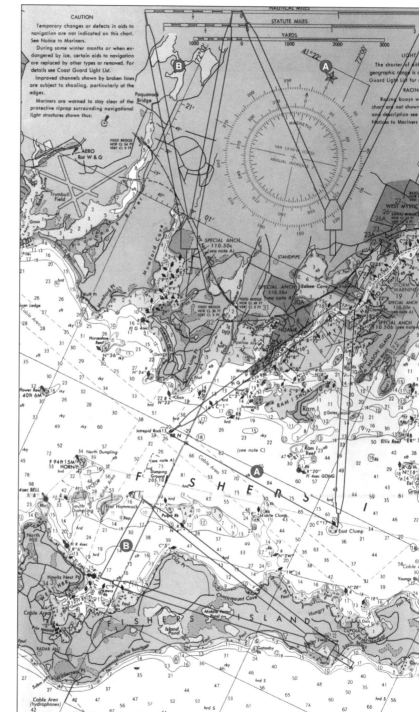, the dividers measure the distance, 2 miles. If you sailed for 20 minutes, your speed would be calculated as 6 knots.

S = $\frac{60 \times \mathbf{D}}{\mathbf{T}}$ = $\frac{60 \times 2 \text{ miles}}{20 \text{ minutes}}$ **S = 6 knots**

Calculating Time

In this case you know your speed is 6 knots, and the dividers measure the distance for **B** as 0.9 miles.

T = $\frac{60 \times \mathbf{D}}{\mathbf{S}}$ = $\frac{60 \times 0.9 \text{ miles}}{6 \text{ knots}}$ **T = 9 minutes**

Calculating Distance

If you have been sailing for 20 minutes at a speed of 6 knots, the distance sailed is 2 miles.

D= $\frac{\mathbf{S} \times \mathbf{T}}{60}$ = $\frac{6 \text{ knots} \times 20 \text{ minutes}}{60}$ **D = 2 miles**

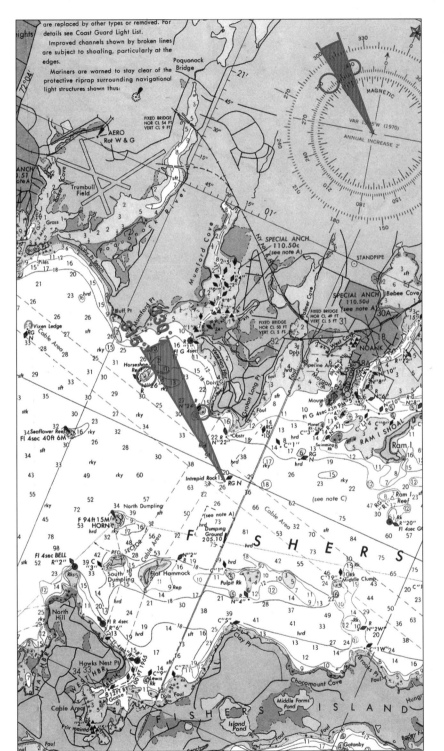

Danger Bearings

A chart, like a road map, shows you potential hazards. If you want to go to Mumford Cove from Intrepid Rock, the chart shows two hazards (*circled*), each marked with buoys that are near your course. Drawing a line from Intrepid Rock to the edge of each hazard, and transferring them to the compass rose, shows the bearings to the hazards are 315 degrees and 330 degrees. These are your danger bearings, and the shaded area marked on the chart in between the bearings is the safe area to sail in.

Hypothermia, Seasickness and Heat Emergencies

Sailing can expose you to extreme conditions, both hot and cold. On hot windless days, you'll be exposed to a lot of sun. On windy, overcast days, the cool spray coming over the bow can send a chill down your spine. Be prepared for these changes. Drink lots of water and wear clothing that protects your skin and head from the sun when it's hot. Have warm clothing along in case the weather turns foul. Put on your jacket or pants before you get cold. In addition, you should know the warning signals for heat and cold emergencies and what to do in those situations.

SEASICKNESS

Sailing can cause motion sickness. You can reduce your chances of becoming seasick by getting plenty of sleep the night before you go sailing.
- Eat before going out, but avoid greasy, heavy foods and alcohol.
- Dress warmly.
- Some people use wrist bands that activate accupressure points. Others rely on prescription medications such as Scopolamine ear patches.
- Symptoms include yawning, burping, paleness, a headache or nausea . Get on deck for fresh air and watch the horizon to calm your sensory system. Better yet, steer the boat. Eating salted crackers or drinking a carbonated cola drink might help. In really bad cases, lie on your back in a spot where you're sheltered from cold and spray.

HYPOTHERMIA

SIGNALS...
- Shivering
- Impaired judgment
- Dizziness
- Numbness
- Confusion
- Weakness
- Impaired vision
- Drowsiness

(Physical symptoms may vary, since age, body size, and clothing will cause individual differences.)

TREATMENT...
Medical assistance should be given to anyone with hypothermia. Until medical assistance arrives, these steps should be taken:
- Move the person to a warm place and handle gently.
- Remove all wet clothing.
- Warm the body temperature gradually.
- Cover person with blankets or sleeping bags and insulate from cold.
- If the person is fully conscious and can swallow, give him or her something warm (not hot), such as warm broth or gelatin. If the person is not fully conscious, don't give any food or drinks.

HEAT STROKE

SIGNALS...
- Hot, red skin
- Constricted pupils
- Very high body temperature
- Skin will feel dry, unless the person is sweating from exertion

TREATMENT...
Heat stroke is life threatening. Anyone afflicted with heat stroke needs to be cooled down while a doctor or EMS technician is contacted immediately.
- Move person to cool environment.
- Cool person in cold bath or by wrapping wet towels or sheets around body.
- Contact a doctor or EMS (Emergency Medical Services) personnel.
- Do not give person anything to eat or drink.

HEAT EXHAUSTION

SIGNALS...
- Cool, pale, moist skin
- Heavy sweating
- Dilated pupils
- Headache
- Dizziness
- Nausea
- Vomiting

TREATMENT
Heat exhaustion is less dangerous than heat stroke. First aid includes the following steps:
- Move person to cool environment.
- Care for shock by placing person on back with feet elevated 8 to 12 inches.
- Remove or loosen clothing.
- Apply wet towels or sheets.
- Give person half a glass of cool water every 15 minutes, if fully conscious and able to tolerate it.

On-Deck Safety

The old adage for sailors - "one hand for the ship, one hand for yourself" - still applies. When the boat heels, rolls and pitches, keep a firm handhold as you make your way around the deck. Keep your center of gravity low by squatting or even getting down on your hands and knees as you move. Consider the lifelines around the boat as a temporary restraint and not an impenetrable barrier! If you get caught in a thunderstorm, avoid touching the mast and shrouds, and any other metal or electrical components aboard your boat in the unlikely event of getting struck by lightning.

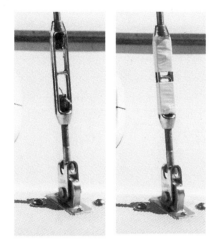

Make sure the sharp ends of cotter pins are turned back and taped to prevent injury.

When wires fray, they create **"fishhooks"** which can cut your hands or tear the sails. Check your halyards and lifelines frequently.

Also, sloppy lines at the base of the mast can become jammed if you have to lower sails in an emergency.

When moving around on deck remember..."**One hand for the boat, and one hand for yourself**"

Sturdy line or wire (*jacklines*) secured to the boat give you a place to hook in with your safety harness tether and move about the deck.

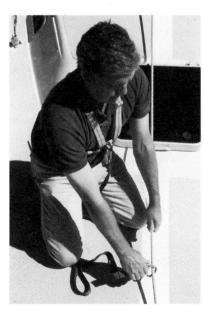

Don't put yourself in a danger zone. If the fairlead breaks (above), this crew member could be injured when the sheet snaps free.

Overboard Recovery

All sailors must know how to react quickly to a crew overboard situation. Losing sight of the victim correlates very highly with loss of life. The Quick-Stop recovery method was developed specifically to eliminate this element of the problem in large offshore boats. It is the preferred method. All of the following recovery methods involve six key elements:

1. *Getting buoyancy to the victim.*
2. *Keeping the victim in sight.*
3. *Heading the boat back to the victim.*
4. *Stopping the boat alongside the victim.*
5. *Making contact with the victim.*
6. *Getting the victim back on board.*

Quick-Stop Recovery

The hallmark of the Quick-Stop recovery method is the immediate reduction of boat speed by turning in a direction to windward and thereafter maneuvering at modest speed, remaining near the victim. This is superior to the conventional procedure of reaching off, then either jibing or tacking and returning on a reciprocal course, since the victim is kept in sight throughout. This recovery requires these steps:

❶ As soon as a crew member falls overboard, throw buoyant objects, such as cushions, PFDs or life rings, to the victim and shout "Crew overboard!" These objects may not only come to the aid of the victim, but will "litter the water" where he or she went overboard and help the spotter to keep him or her in view. It has been determined that the deployment of the standard overboard pole rig requires too much time. The pole rig is saved to "put on top" of the person in case the initial maneuver is unsuccessful.

❷ Designate someone to spot and point at the person in the water. The spotter should NEVER take his or her eyes off the victim.

❸ Bring the boat into the wind, trimming the mainsail to close-hauled.

❹ Continue to turn through the wind, without releasing the headsail, until the wind is almost astern. Do not ease the sails.

❺ Hold this course until the victim is aft of the beam, and drop or furl the headsail if possible. If the headsail is lowered, its sheets should not be slacked.

❻ Jibe the boat.

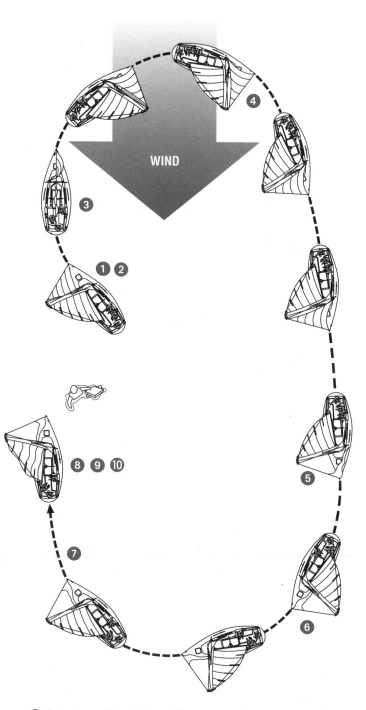

❼ Steer toward the victim as if you were going to pick up a mooring.

❽ Stop the boat alongside the victim by easing or backing sails.

❾ Establish contact with the victim with a heaving line or other device. A "throwing sock" containing 75 feet of light floating line and a kapok bag can be thrown into the wind because the line is kept inside the bag and trails out as it sails to the victim.

❿ Recover the victim on board.

This method should be executed under sail alone unless there is insufficient wind to maneuver the boat.

Lifesling-Type Recovery

If there are few people on board, the Lifesling-type recovery method should be employed. It takes longer than the Quick-Stop, but provides a means for a single crew member to effect a rescue of a victim in the water. This recovery requires these steps:

1 As soon as a crew member falls overboard, throw a cushion or other buoyant objects to the victim and shout "Crew-overboard!" while the boat is brought IMMEDIATELY head-to-wind, slowed and stopped. The main is trimmed to centerline.

2 The Lifesling is deployed by opening the bag that is hung on the stern pulpit and dropping the sling into the water. It will trail out astern and draw out the remaining line.

3 Once deployed, the boat is sailed in a wide circle around the victim with the line and sling trailing astern. The jib is not tended but allowed to back from the head-to-wind position, which increases the rate of turn.

4 Contact is established with the victim by the line and sling being drawn inward by the boat's circling motion.

The Lifesling is a floating device attached to the boat by a length of floating line that doubles as a hoisting sling to retrieve a victim in the water. If the side of the boat is too high to reach the victim, or the victim is injured, the sling can be used to hoist the person up and over the lifelines.

The victim then places the sling over his or her head and under his or her arms.

5 Upon contact, the boat is put head-to-wind again, the headsail is dropped to the deck or furled and the main is doused.

6 As the boat drifts, the crew begins pulling the sling and the victim to the boat. If necessary, a cockpit winch can be used to assist in this phase, which should continue until the victim is alongside and pulled up tightly until he or she is suspended in the sling (so that he or she will not drop out).

This system is effective if: 1) line length is preadjusted to avoid running over the line, and 2) method is practiced to complete competence.

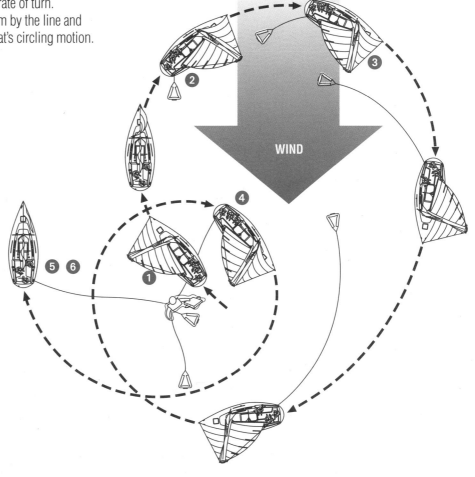

Quick-Turn Recovery

For small inshore keelboats whose stability characteristics may result in loss of control during a jibe in heavy weather, the Quick-Turn (or Figure-8) recovery allows for a return to the victim without jibing. Take the following steps in a Quick-Turn recovery:

1. As soon as a crew member falls overboard, throw buoyant objects, such as cushions, PFDs or life rings, to the victim and shout "Crew overboard!"
2. Designate someone to spot and point at the person in the water. The spotter should NEVER take his or her eyes off the victim.
3. Sail the boat on a beam reach for a maximum of four boat lengths.
4. Tack into the wind and fall off onto a very broad reach, crossing the boat's original course.
5. When downwind of the victim, turn into the wind as if you were going to pick up a mooring.
6. Stop the boat alongside the victim by easing or backing sails.
7. Establish contact with the victim with a heaving line or other device.
8. Recover the victim on board.

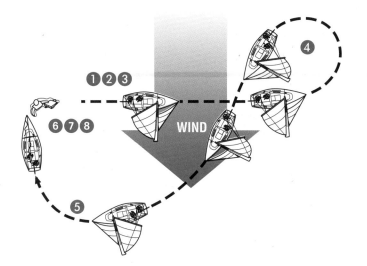

Under Power Recovery

There may be occasions when a quick recovery under sail is not possible. For instance, if you're motoring along under power or there is not enough wind, or in the worst case scenario, the mast has failed and gone overboard, take the following steps:

1. As soon as a crew member falls overboard, throw buoyant objects, such as cushions, PFDs or life rings, to the victim and shout "Crew overboard!"

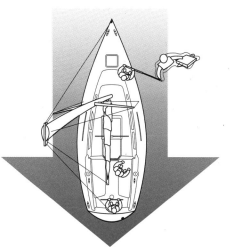

2. Designate someone to spot and point at the person in the water. The spotter should NEVER take his or her eyes off the victim.
3. Return to the victim. If the boat was not under power, make sure all sheets and lines are on board the boat and secured before turning on the engine and putting it into gear. While making the recovery, maintain constant vigilance that no lines go overboard. A line in the water is a serious hazard, since it could get caught in the propeller and thereby disable the boat.
4. Approach the victim with the boat headed into the wind and under very slow speed. Stop the boat alongside the victim.
5. Establish contact with the victim with a heaving line or other device, and put engine in neutral.
6. Recover the victim on board. Make sure the victim does not get near the propeller at any time during the recovery procedure.

Running Aground

It's hard to find sailors who haven't stuck their keel into the mud at least once. Usually, the only damage is a bruised ego, but running aground can be serious if you slam into a rock. You can often get yourself free and sailing again if you know what to do. First, check the bilge of the boat to make sure the impact hasn't caused any leaking. Then figure out if you can simply wait for the incoming tide to lift you off the bottom, or if you have to be more aggressive in freeing yourself.

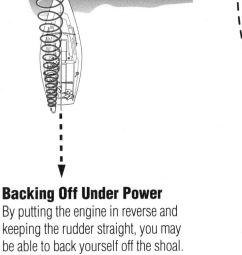

Backing Off Under Power

By putting the engine in reverse and keeping the rudder straight, you may be able to back yourself off the shoal.

Kedging

Using your anchor, you can also pull yourself free (*kedge off*). Use your dinghy to carry the anchor directly astern until you reach a scope of about 5:1. Lead the anchor line to a cockpit sheet winch and grind the line in with the rudder straight.

Heeling Boat

You can decrease the boat's depth (*draft*) by heeling over. Swing the boom out to the side and have members of the crew sit on it. This may free the keel from the bottom.

Fire Safety

Most fires on cruising boats can be traced to fuel leaks or electrical failures. Regulations require sailboats to carry up-to-date fire extinguishers, and for your safety, be sure you know where they are located and how to operate them.

Multi-purpose Dry Chemical A,B,C is a universal extinguisher which can be used on all fires.

NOTE: Do not touch the discharging horn of the CO_2 extinguisher because of extreme cold.

Combustion occurs when three ingredients are present.

Fuel feeds a fire. On a boat this fuel can be diesel, gasoline, propane, fiberglass, or wood, among other things.

FUEL

The flame from a match or the spark from a short circuit provide the heat to ignite a fire. Insulation on wire prevents short circuits.

THE FIRE TRIANGLE

AIR

HEAT

Air feeds a fire. Remove air to smother it. Certain fire extinguishers discharge chemicals that take away the oxygen,

Types of fires	Extinguishers
Ordinary combustibles (wood, paper, cloth, rubber, and many plastics)	Water, and multi-purpose Dry Chemical extinguishers labeled A,B,C or Halon labeled A can be used.
Fuel fires	Carbon Dioxide (CO_2), Dry Chemical or Halon extinguishers can be used to extinguish fuel fires. Never use water for fuel fires except alcohol stoves.
Electrical fires	CO_2, Dry Chemical and Halon extinguishers can be used even when electricity is on.
Engine compartment	CO_2, Dry Chemical or Halon extinguishers should be discharged into the compartment through a small opening. Never open the compartment where a fire is burning.

Wheel
Turning the wheel turns the sprocket and chain which moves the steering cables.

Pedestal
Inside the pedestal, the wheel has a sprocket and chain to which the steering cables are attached.

Sheave
Check the sheaves for wearing or chafe by looking for signs of metal particles.

Emergency Tiller

Steering Failure
Inspections prevent most potential steering problems. For example, chafe and broken strands will cause the wire steering cables of a wheel system to fail, but regular inspections will detect this so you can make repairs before there is a problem. Inspections allow you to become familiar with what is normal and recognize the unusual.

NOTE: If you have a steering failure, your emergency tiller is there to back you up. Make sure you know where it's stowed and how to attach it to the rudder post.

Sheave
Each cable runs from the pedestal through a sheave under the cockpit sole.

Steering Cable
Check the cable for binding, fraying, tension and perfect alignment.

Quadrant
The quadrant connects the steering cables to the rudder post and turns in response to the pulling of the cables.

Rudder Post
The rudder post extends above the quadrant for the emergency tiller.

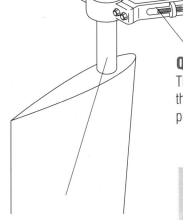

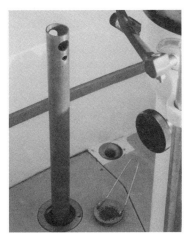

Remove the access plate above the top of the rudder post to install the emergency tiller.

Towing

In some emergencies, such as being hard aground or suffering a broken engine, you may have to request or accept a tow from another boat. Use a strong line like your anchor rode and attach it to a strong part of your boat. Start the tow slowly. Increase the length of the towing line as you increase speed.

You can tie a bowline around the mast at deck level for a strong connection. Do not do this if the mast is stepped on the deck, however!

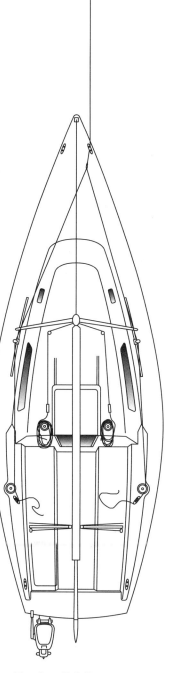

Towing Bridle

Tie a bowline in the end of the towing line at the foredeck and lead another strong line through it, anchoring each end on the jib winches in the cockpit.

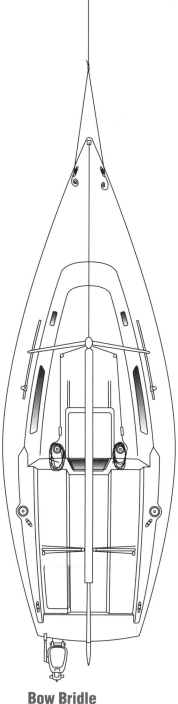

Bow Bridle

Divide the load on the towline by leading a bridle from the end of the towline to two cleats on the foredeck. Make sure the cleats are through-bolted to substantial backing plates in order to carry the load.

Flooding

A broken window (*port*) or hatch or a hole in the hull can flood your boat. Your bilge pump will help remove the water, and you may have to use buckets to bail by hand if the situation becomes serious. Cover a window or a hatch by screwing, nailing or tying on pieces of wood, which can sometimes be found under your mattresses or the cabin sole. For holes in the hull, tie a mattress or a sail over the puncture on the outside. Use cushions, sail bags or clothing to plug the opening from the inside.

▶ If possible, heel the boat over so that the hole stays above water.

▶ Make sure the water in the bilge contains no small debris, such as wood, fiberglass, paint or dirt, that will clog the pump's intake.

▶ If you're in danger of sinking, make sure everyone on board is wearing a PFD and knows the procedure for abandoning ship, including how to make an emergency broadcast on VHF.

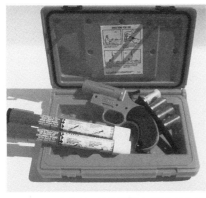

Flares can be hand-held or shot into the air with a special gun to signal distress.

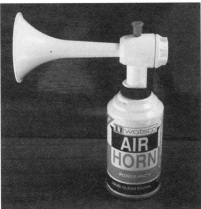

You can also call for help by repeatedly blasting an air horn to attract attention.

Signaling for Help

Before you decide to ask for outside assistance, determine if you can take care of the problem yourself. You may be able to get back to the harbor under your own power, or accept a tow from a friendly boat. Coast Guard and private search-and-rescue missions are expensive and time-consuming. If you do need to signal for help, use the signals, either separately or together, that are recognized by the Coast Guard and the Navigation Rules.

International Distress Signals

▶ A smoke signal giving off orange-colored smoke.

▶ A rocket parachute flare or a hand flare showing a red light.

▶ Rockets or shells, throwing red stars fired one at a time at short intervals.

▶ Flashlight or other device signaling SOS (*dot-dot-dot, dash-dash-dash, dot-dot-dot*) in the Morse Code.

▶ Continuous sounding of a foghorn.

▶ Flames, such as a fire in a bucket or barrel.

▶ "Mayday" spoken over a radiotelephone.

▶ A signal consisting of a square flag having above or below it a ball or anything resembling a ball.

▶ Flying the international code flags or signals "N" and "C".

▶ Firing a gun or other explosive device at intervals of about a minute.

▶ Slowly and repeatedly waving both outstretched arms.

▶ A high intensity white light flashing at regular intervals from 50 to 70 times per minute.

▶ A radiotelegraph or radiotelephone alarm signal.

▶ Signals transmitted by an emergency position-indicating radio beacon (EPIRB).

Safety Equipment

The U.S. Coast Guard requires sailboats to carry certain safety equipment. If you're not sure that you have all the items you need to meet the official requirements, you can obtain the pamphlet entitled "Federal Requirements for Recreational Boats" from your local chandlery, USCG stations or by writing US Coast Guard, 2100 Second St. SW, Washington, DC 20593. Listed here is a summary of the minimum required safety gear, which should be supplemented by the boat owner. Also, local governments may have their own safety requirements to which you should comply.

▶ USCG approved Personal Flotation Devices (PFDs) of Type I, II, III, or V are required for each person aboard the vessel. At least one Type IV (throwable) must also be on board. The PFDs need to be readily accessible and of the appropriate size for passengers on the boat. The Type IV PFD must be immediately available while underway.

▶ All boats longer than 16 feet should have a high-pitched whistle or horn and all boats 39 feet and longer must have a power whistle or horn with a range of at least 1/2 mile or more (*for larger vessels*), as well as a bell.

▶ USCG approved Visual Distress Signals must be carried by all boats except those that are: less than 16 feet in length, participating in organized events such as regattas, open sailboats less than 26 feet in length

A radar reflector hung in the boat's rigging will alert other vessels of your presence in periods of restricted visibility.

without auxiliary power or manually propelled boats. Don't display any of these signals unless you need emergency assistance.

▶ USCG approved fire extinguishers must be carried aboard all auxiliary powered vessels.

▶ Boats less than 26 feet long must have one Type B-1. Boats 26 to 40 feet long must have two Type B-1s or one Type B-2.

▶ Navigation lights must be displayed between sunset and sunrise while underway or anchored.

▶ A boat sailing and being propelled by an engine at the same time (motorsailing) must display, where it can best be seen, an inverted conical shape. (Boats less than 12 meters long are exempted from this requirement.)

▶ Boats with inboard gasoline engines must have flame arrestors. Most boats with auxiliary engines must also be ventilated.

▶ During the day, sailboats at anchor shall exhibit forward, where best seen, a ball shape.

▶ Vessels restricted in their ability to maneuver because of diving operations or activity must display a rigid replica of the code flag "A".

Recommended Safety Gear

▶ Additional means of propulsion, including oars, paddles or an outboard motor.

▶ Manual bailing devices, such as buckets or bilge pumps.

▶ A basic first aid kit with instructions.

▶ An anchor and anchor line.

▶ A radar reflector.

▶ A tool kit, spare parts and through-hull plugs.

▶ A portable VHF radio.

▶ Navigation charts and compass.

▶ Lifesling, a flotation device with attached line for retrieving crew from the water. Especially useful when sailing with just one or two crew.

Federal Safety Requirements

The U.S. Coast Guard is the federal law enforcement agency for boating. When you are sailing and are hailed by a Coast Guard vessel, you are required to heave-to or drop sails so that an inspection officer may board. Other local, state or federal law enforcement agencies may also board and examine your boat.

Each U.S. Coast Guard vessel has a distinctive stripe on the hull and the words "Coast Guard" on the side of the vessel. There are uniformed, armed Coast Guard personnel aboard each vessel.

Boarding Inspection

A Coast Guard boarding officer finding a boat operating in an unsafe condition may require it to return to port immediately. Conditions that may cause termination of use are:
▶ Insufficient Coast Guard Approved Personal Flotation Devices (PFDs)
▶ Insufficient fire extinguishers
▶ Overloaded conditions, i.e. exceeds listing on the capacity plate or obviously inadequate for the number of people on board.
▶ Improper navigation light display
▶ Fuel leakage
▶ Fuel in bilges
▶ Improper ventilation
▶ Improper backfire flame control
▶ Manifestly unsafe voyage, i.e. unsafe vessel, weather conditions, or hazardous situation which could result in injury or death, or require rescue.

Additional Basic Regulations

▶ Operating a boat under the influence of drugs or alcohol may result in a civil penalty or a criminal action.
▶ Negligent or Grossly Negligent Operation of a vessel which endangers lives and property is prohibited by law.
▶ Improper use of a radiotelephone (VHF) is a criminal offense.
▶ Boating accidents should be reported to the nearest state authority per the federal requirement.
▶ You are obligated to render as much assistance as can be safely provided to anyone in danger at sea.

The Float Plan

Before you leave for a day of sailing, it is a good idea to tell someone else your plans. Leave a float plan with a friend or relative who can contact the Coast Guard or other agencies in the event you don't return on schedule. The following information should be included:

▶ Name and phone number of the person reporting: *Peter James, 413-5234.*
▶ Complete description of the boat including type, color, registration number, sail number or insignia, length, etc: *sailboat, sloop rig, white hull, light blue deck, CF0067 LK, Sail #4546, 30-foot, "Snoopy."*
▶ List of people on board including name, age, address & phone: *Bob James, 38, Susie James, 35, Eric James, 10, all live at 436 Walnut St, Livermore, 446-2141.*
▶ Radio type and call sign: VHF - WRS 9821.
▶ Survival gear aboard: *4 PFDs, 1 Lifesling, 3 smoke flares.*
▶ Trip Plan: Leaving at *0800* from *Marina Village, Pier 8* going to *Angel Island.* Expect to return by *1700* and in no event later than *2000.*
▶ If not returned by *2200* call the U.S.Coast Guard or Police at 911.

Rig Types

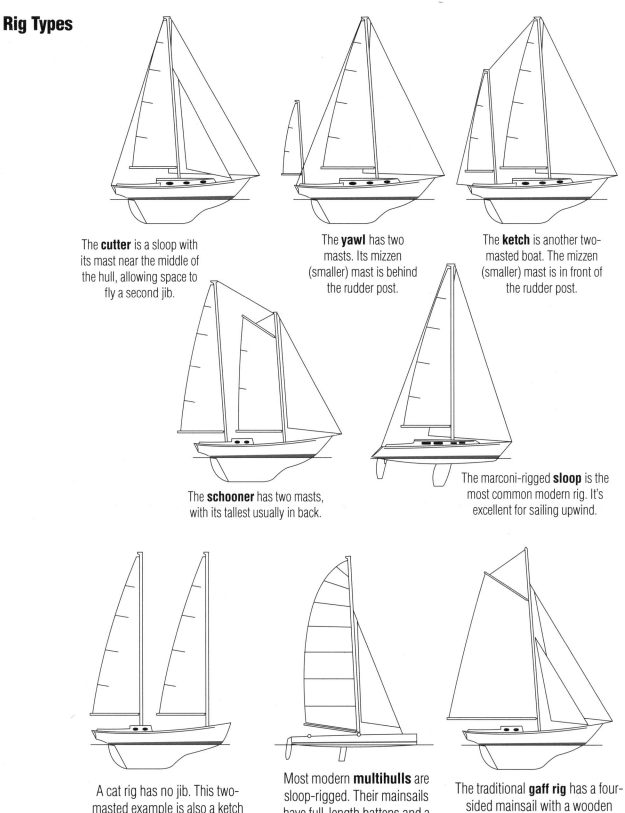

The **cutter** is a sloop with its mast near the middle of the hull, allowing space to fly a second jib.

The **yawl** has two masts. Its mizzen (smaller) mast is behind the rudder post.

The **ketch** is another two-masted boat. The mizzen (smaller) mast is in front of the rudder post.

The **schooner** has two masts, with its tallest usually in back.

The marconi-rigged **sloop** is the most common modern rig. It's excellent for sailing upwind.

A cat rig has no jib. This two-masted example is also a ketch rig. Hence the name **cat ketch**.

Most modern **multihulls** are sloop-rigged. Their mainsails have full-length battens and a large curved roach (leech).

The traditional **gaff rig** has a four-sided mainsail with a wooden spar (gaff) attached to the top.

Hull Types

A monohull is a boat with a single hull.

The twin-hulled catamaran features speed and stability.

The three-hulled trimaran can also carry a lot of sail for speed.

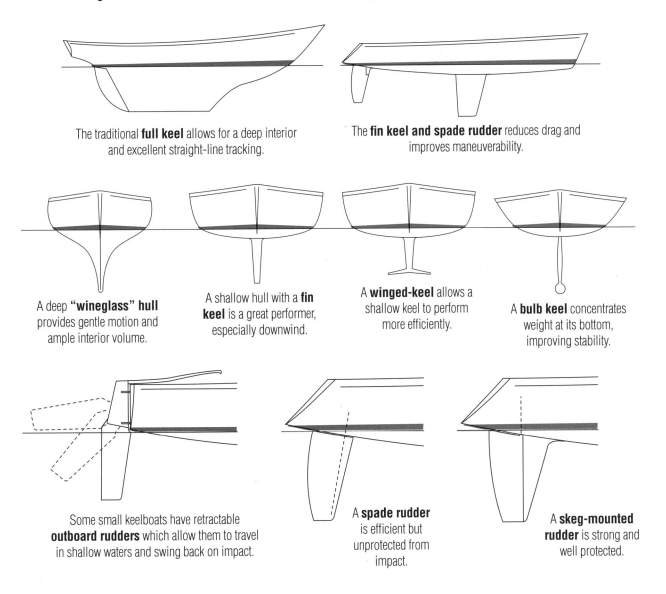

The traditional **full keel** allows for a deep interior and excellent straight-line tracking.

The **fin keel and spade rudder** reduces drag and improves maneuverability.

A deep **"wineglass" hull** provides gentle motion and ample interior volume.

A shallow hull with a **fin keel** is a great performer, especially downwind.

A **winged-keel** allows a shallow keel to perform more efficiently.

A **bulb keel** concentrates weight at its bottom, improving stability.

Some small keelboats have retractable **outboard rudders** which allow them to travel in shallow waters and swing back on impact.

A **spade rudder** is efficient but unprotected from impact.

A **skeg-mounted rudder** is strong and well protected.

A

Abeam - off the side of (at right angle to) the boat.

Aboard - on the boat.

Adrift - a boat drifting without control.

Aft - at or toward the stern or behind the boat.

Aground - a boat whose keel is touching the bottom.

Alternator - a device which generates electricity from an engine.

Amidships - toward the center of the boat.

Apparent wind - the wind aboard a moving boat.

Astern - behind the stern of the boat.

Athwartships - across the boat from side to side.

B

Backstay - the standing rigging running from the stern to the top of the mast, keeping the mast from falling forward.

Back - 1.- to stop or to propel a boat backward by holding the clew of a sail out to windward. 2.- a counterclockwise change of wind direction.

Bail - to empty a boat of water.

Ballast - weight in the keel of a boat that provides stability.

Barometer - a weather forecasting instrument that measures air pressure.

Batten - a thin slat that slides into a pocket in the leech of a sail, helping it hold its shape.

Battery - storage chamber for electricity.

Battery switch - the main electrical cutoff switch.

Beam - the width of a boat at its widest point.

Beam reach (point of sail) sailing in a direction at approximately 90 degrees to the wind.

Bear away - to fall off, head away from the wind.

Bearing - the direction from one object to another expressed in compass degrees.

Beating - a course sailed upwind.

Below - the area of a boat beneath the deck.

Bend - to attach a sail to a spar or a headstay, or to attach a line to a sail.

Berth - 1. - the area in which you park your boat; 2. - the area in which you sleep on a boat.

Bight - a loop in a line.

Bilge - the lowest part of the boat's interior, where water on board will collect.

Bitter end - the end of a line.

Blanket - to use a sail or object to block the wind from filling a sail.

Block - a pulley on a boat.

Boat hook - a pole with a hook on the end used for grabbing hold of a mooring or retrieving something that has fallen overboard.

Boat speed - the speed of a boat through the water.

Bolt rope - the rope sewn into the foot and luff of some mainsails and the luff of some jibs by which the sails are attached to the boat.

Boom - the spar extending directly aft from the mast to which the foot of the mainsail is attached

Boom vang - a block and tackle system which pulls the boom down to assist sail control.

Bottom - 1. - the underside of the boat. 2. - the land under the water.

Bow - the forward part of the boat.

Bow line (BOW - line) - a line running from the bow of the boat to the dock or mooring.

Bowline - (BOE-lin) - a knot designed to make a loop that will not slip and can be easily untied.

Breast line - a short dockline leading off the beam of the boat directly to the dock.

Broach - an uncontrolled rounding up into the wind, usually from a downwind point of sail.

Broad reach - (point of sail) sailing in a direction with the wind at the rear corner of the boat (approximately 135 degrees from the bow).

Bulkhead - a wall that runs athwartships on a boat, usually providing structural support to the hull.

Bunk - see **berth**, definition #2

Buoy - a floating navigation marker.

Buoyancy - the ability of an object to float.

By the lee - sailing on a run with the wind coming over the same side of the boat as the boom.

C

Cabin - the interior of a boat.

Can - an odd-numbered, green buoy marking the left side of a channel as you return to port.

Capsize - to tip or turn a boat over.

Cast off - to release a line when leaving a dock or mooring.

Catamaran - a twin-hulled sailing vessel with a deck or trampoline between the hulls.

Catboat - a boat with only a mainsail and the mast located at the bow.

Centerline - the midline of a boat running from bow to stern.

Center of Effort - the focal point of the force of the wind on the sails.

Center of Lateral Resistance - the focal point of the force of the water on the underbody of the boat.

Chafe - wear on a line or wire caused by rubbing.

Chainplates - strong metal plates which connect the shrouds to the boat.

Channel - a (usually narrow) path in the water, marked by buoys, in which the water is deep enough to sail.

Chart - a nautical map.

Charter - to rent a boat.

Chock - a guide mounted on the deck through which docklines and anchor rode are run.

Choke - a device for controlling the mixture of air and fuel for an engine.

Chop - rough, short, steep waves.

Cleat - a nautical fitting that is used to secure a line.

Clew - the lower, aft corner of a sail. The clew of the mainsail is held taut by the outhaul. The jib sheets are attached to the clew of the jib.

Close-hauled - the point of sail that is closest to the wind.

Close reach - (point of sail) sailing in a direction with the wind forward of the beam (about 70 degrees from the bow).

Coaming - the short protective wall surrounding the cockpit.

Cockpit - the lower area in which the steering controls and sail controls are located.

Coil - to loop a line neatly so it can be stored.

Come about - see **tack**.

Companionway - the steps leading from the cockpit or deck to the cabin below.

Compass - the magnetic instrument which indicates the direction in which the boat is headed.

Compass protractor - a plotting instrument oriented to latitude-longitude lines.

Compass rose - the twin circles on a chart which indicate the direction of true north and magnetic north.

Course - the direction in which the boat is steered.

Crew - besides the skipper, anyone on board who helps sail the boat.

Cringle - a ring sewn into the sail through which a line can be passed.

Cunningham - a line running through a grommet about eight inches up from the tack of a mainsail that is used to tighten the luff of the sail.

Current - the horizontal movement of water caused by tides, wind and other forces.

Cutter - a single-masted boat with the mast near the middle that is capable of flying both a jib and a staysail.

D

Daysailer - a small sailboat.

Dead downwind - sailing in a direction straight downwind.

Deck - the mostly flat surface area on top of the boat.

Deck plate - a covered opening on deck leading to the water or fuel tanks, used for pumping out the holding tank or for access to the rudder post in case you need to install the emergency tiller.

Depower - to release the power from the sails by allowing them to luff or making them flatter. This is done to reduce heel.

Dinghy - a small sailboat or rowboat.

Displacement - the weight of a boat; therefore the amount of water it displaces.

Divider - instrument used for measuring distances or coordinates on a chart.

Dock - 1. - the wooden structure where a boat may be tied up. 2. - the act of bringing the boat to rest alongside the structure.

Dockline - a line used to secure the boat to the dock.

Dodger - a canvas protection in front of the cockpit of some boats that is designed to keep spray off the skipper and crew.

Downhaul - a line used to pull down on the movable gooseneck on some boats to tighten the luff of the mainsail. The cunningham has the same function on other boats.

Downwind - away from the direction of the wind.

Draft - the depth of a boat's keel from the water's surface.

E

Ease - to let out a line or sail.

Ebb - an outgoing tide.

EPIRB - Emergency Position-Indicating Radio Beacon

F

Fairlead - a fitting that guides a jib sheet or other lines back to the cockpit or along the deck.

Fairway - the center of a channel.

Fall off - see **head down**.

Fast - secured.

Fathom - a measurement of the depth of water. One fathom equals six feet.

Fender - a rubber bumper used to protect a boat by keeping it from hitting a dock.

Fend off - push off.

Fetch - a course on which a boat can make its destination without having to tack.

Fishhooks - frayed wire that can cut your skin or rip sails.

Fitting - a piece of nautical hardware.

Flake - to lay out a line on deck using large loops to keep it from becoming tangled.

Flood - an incoming tide.

Float plan - an itinerary of your intended sailing

trip, left with a responsible party onshore.

Following sea - waves hitting the boat from astern.

Foot - the bottom edge of a sail.

Fore - forward.

Forepeak - a storage area in the bow (below the deck).

Foresail - a jib or a genoa.

Forestay - the standing rigging running from the bow to the mast to which the jib is hanked on.

Forward - toward the bow.

Fouled - tangled.

Foul-weather gear - water-resistant clothing.

Freeboard - the height of the hull above the water's surface.

Full - not luffing.

Furl - to fold or roll up a sail.

G

Gaff - on some boats, a spar along the top edge of a four-sided sail.

Gear - generic term for sailing equipment.

Genoa - a large jib whose clew extends aft of the mast.

Give-way vessel - the vessel required to give way to another boat when they may be on a collision course.

Glide zone - the distance a sailboat takes to coast to a stop.

Gooseneck - the strong fitting that connects the boom to the mast.

Grommet - a reinforcing metal ring set in a sail.

Ground tackle - the anchor and rode (chain and line).

Gudgeon - a fitting attached to the stern of a boat into which the pintles of a rudder are inserted.

Gunwale (GUNN-nle) - the edge of the deck where it meets the topsides.

Gust - see **puff**.

H

Halyard - a line used to hoist or lower a sail.

Hank - a snap hook that is used to connect the luff of a jib onto the forestay.

"Hard a-lee" - the command given to the crew just prior to tacking.

Hard over - to turn the tiller or wheel as far as possible in one direction.

Hatch - a large covered opening in the deck.

Hatch boards - boards that close off the companionway.

Haul in - to tighten a line.

Head - 1. - the top corner of a sail. 2. - the bathroom on a boat. 3. - the toilet on a boat.

Headboard - the reinforcing small board affixed to the head of a sail.

Header - a wind shift which makes your boat head down or sails to be sheeted in.

Heading - the direction of the boat expressed in compass degrees.

Head down - to fall off, changing course away from the wind.

Head off - see **head down**.

Head up - to come up, changing course toward the wind.

Headsail - a jib, genoa, or staysail.

Headstay - the standing rigging running from the bow to the mast.

Head-to-wind - the course of the boat when the bow is dead into the wind.

Headway - progress made forward.

Heave - to throw.

Heave-to - to hold one's position in the water by using the force of the sails and rudder to counter one another.

Heavy weather - strong winds and large waves.

Heel - the lean of a boat caused by the wind.

Helm - the tiller or wheel.

Helmsman - the person responsible for steering the boat.

High side - the windward side of the boat.

Hike - to position crew members out over the windward rail to help balance the boat.

Hiking stick - see **tiller extension**.

Holding ground - the bottom ground in an anchorage used to hold the anchor.

Hove-to - a boat that has completed the process of heaving-to, with its jib aback, its main loosely trimmed, and its rudder securely positioned to steer it close to the wind.

Hull - the body of the boat, excluding rig and sails.

Hull speed - the theoretical maximum speed of a sailboat determined by the length of its waterline.

I

Inboard - inside of the rail of a boat.

In irons - a boat that is head-to-wind, making no forward headway.

J

Jacklines - sturdy wire, rope or webbing securely fastened at its ends on deck which permits the crew to hook in with their safety harnesses.

Jib - the small forward sail of a boat attached to the forestay.

Jibe - to change direction of a boat by steering the stern through the wind.

"Jibe-ho" - the command given to the crew when starting a jibe.

Jiffy reef - a quick reefing system allowing a section of the mainsail to be tied to the boom.

Jury rig - an improvised, temporary repair.

K

Kedge off - to use an anchor to pull a boat into deeper water after it has run aground.

Keel - the heavy vertical fin beneath a boat that helps keep it upright and prevents it from slipping sideways in the water.

Ketch - a two-masted boat with its mizzen (after) mast shorter than its mainmast and located forward of the rudder post.

King spoke - a marker on the steering wheel which indicates when the rudder is centered.

Knockdown - a boat heeled so far that one of its spreaders touches the water.

Knot - one nautical mile per hour.

L

Land breeze - a wind that blows over land and out to sea.

Lash - to tie down.

Lay - to sail a course that will clear an obstacle without tacking.

Lazarette - a storage compartment built into the deck.

Lazy sheet - the windward side jib sheet that is not under strain.

Lead (LEED) - to pass a line through a fitting or a block.

Lee helm - the boat's tendency to turn away from the wind.

Lee shore - land which is on the leeward side of the boat. Because the wind is blowing in that direction, a lee shore could pose a danger.

Leech - the after edge of a sail.

Leech line - an adjustable cord sewn into the back edge of a sail to prevent fluttering

Leeward - (LEW-erd) - the direction away from the wind (where the wind is blowing to).

Leeward side - the side of the boat or sail that is away from the wind.

Leeway - sideways slippage of the boat in a direction away from the wind.

Lifeline - plastic coated wire, supported by stanchions, around the outside of the deck to help prevent crew members from falling overboard.

Lifesling - a floating device attached to the boat by a length of floating line that doubles as a hoisting sling to retrieve a victim in the water.

Lift - 1. - the force that results from air passing by a sail, or water past a keel, that moves the boat forward and sideways. 2. - a change in wind direction which lets the boat head up.

Line - a nautical rope.

Line stoppers - levered cleats which hold lines under load and can be released easily.

Low side - the leeward side of the boat.

Lubber's line - a small post in a compass used to help determine a course or a bearing.

Luff - 1. - the forward edge of a sail.
2. - the fluttering of a sail caused by aiming too close to the wind.

Lull - a decrease in wind speed for a short duration.

M

Magnetic - in reference to magnetic north rather than true north.

Mainmast - the taller of two masts on a boat.

Mainsail (MAIN-sil) - the sail hoisted on the mast of a sloop or cutter or the sail hoisted on the mainmast of a ketch or yawl.

Mainsheet - the controlling line for the mainsail.

Marlinspike - a pointed tool used to loosen knots.

Mast - the large aluminum or wooden pole in the middle of a boat from which the mainsail is set.

Master switch - see **battery switch**.

Masthead - the top of the mast.

Masthead fly - a wind direction indicator on top of the mast.

Mast step - the structure that the bottom of the mast sits on.

Mayday - the internationally recognized distress signal for a life-threatening emergency.

Mizzen - the small aftermost sail on a ketch or yawl hoisted on the mizzen mast.

Mooring - a permanently anchored ball or buoy to which a boat can be tied.

MSD - marine sanitation device, including toilet, holding tank and connecting lines and valves.

N

Nautical mile - a distance of 6076 feet, equaling one minute of the earth's latitude.

Navigation Rules - laws established to prevent collisions on the water.

No-Go Zone - an area into the wind in which a boat cannot produce power to sail.

Nun - a red, even-numbered buoy, marking the right side of a channel as you return to port. Nuns are usually paired with cans.

O

Offshore wind - wind blowing off (away from) the

land.

Offshore - away from or out of sight of land.

Off the wind - sailing downwind.

On the wind - sailing upwind, close-hauled.

Outboard - outside the rail of a boat.

Outhaul - the controlling line attached to the clew of a mainsail used to tension the foot of the sail.

Overpowered - a boat that is heeling too far because it has too much sail up for the amount of wind.

Overtaking - a boat that is catching up to another boat and about to pass it.

P

Packing gland - see **stuffing box**.

Painter - the line attached to the bow of a dinghy.

Pan- the internationally recognized distress signal for an urgent situation.

Parallel rulers - two rulers linked and held parallel by hinges.

Pay out - to ease a line.

PFD - abbreviation for Personal Flotation Device, a life jacket.

Piling - vertical timber or log driven into the sea bottom to support docks or form a breakwater.

Pinching - sailing too close to the wind.

Pintle - small metal extensions on a rudder that slides into a gudgeon on the transom. The gudgeon/pintle fitting allows the rudder to swing back and forth.

Plot - applying calculations to a chart to determine course or position.

Point - to steer close to the wind.

Points of sail - boat directions in relation to wind direction, i.e., close-hauled, beam reaching, broad reaching, and running.

Port - 1. - the left side of a boat when facing forward. 2. - a harbor. 3. - a window in a cabin on a boat.

Port tack - sailing on any point of sail with the wind coming over the port side of the boat.

Prevailing wind - typical or consistent wind conditions.

Propeller - a device, having a revolving hub with radiating blades, which is used for propulsion.

Puff - an increase in wind speed for a short duration.

Pulpit - a stainless steel guardrail at the bow and stern of some boats.

Pushpit - a stainless steel guardrail at the stern of some boats.

Push-pull principle - the explanation of how sails generate power.

Q

Quarter - the sides of the boat near the stern.

Quarter berth - a bunk located under the cockpit

R

Radar reflector - a metal object with lots of faces at sharp angles which can be spotted by other vessels' radar scopes.

Rail - the outer edges of the deck.

Rake - the angle of the mast.

Range - the alignment of two objects that indicate the middle of a channel.

Raw-water - the fresh or salt water in which the boat floats.

Reach - one of several points of sail across the wind.

"Ready about" - the command given to the crew to prepare to tack.

"Ready to jibe" - the command given to the crew to prepare to jibe.

Reef - to reduce the size of a sail.

Reefing line - a line used to reduce sail by pulling the lower portion of the sail to the boom.

Reeve - to pass a line through a cringle or block.

Rhumb line - a straight course between two points.

Rig - 1. - the design of a boat's mast(s), standing rigging, and sail plan. 2. - to prepare a boat to go sailing.

Rigging - the wires and lines used to support and control sails.

Right-of-way - the right of the stand-on vessel to hold its course.

Roach - the sail area aft of a straight line running from the head to the clew of a sail.

Rode - line and chain attached from the boat to the anchor.

Roller furling - a mechanical system to roll up a headsail (jib) around the headstay.

Round up - when the boat turns, sometimes abruptly and with a great deal of heel, towards the wind.

Rudder - the underwater fin that is controlled by the tiller to deflect water and steer the boat.

Run - (point of sail) sailing with the wind coming directly behind the boat.

Running rigging - lines and hardware used to control the sails.

S

Safety harness - strong webbing worn around the chest and attached to the boat to prevent someone from being separated from the boat.

Sail cover - the protective cover used to preserve sails when they are not in use.

Sail ties - pieces of line or webbing used to tie the

mainsail to the boom when reefing or storing the sail.

Schooner - a two-masted boat whose foremast is shorter than its mainmast.

Scope - the ratio of the amount of anchor rode deployed to the distance from the bow to the bottom.

Scull - to propel a boat by swinging the rudder back and forth.

Scupper - cockpit or deck drain.

Seabag - a soft-fabric bag for carrying personal items.

Sea breeze - a wind that blows over the sea and onto the land.

Seacock - a valve which opens and closes a hole through the hull for salt water needed on board or discharge.

Secure - make safe or cleat.

Sécurite- an internationally recognized signal to warn others of a dangerous situation.

Set - 1. the direction of a current. 2. to trim the sails.

Shackle - a metal fitting at the end of a line used to attach the line to a sail or another fitting.

Shake out - to remove a reef and restore the full sail.

Sheave - the rotating wheel inside a block or fitting.

Sheet - the line which is used to control the sail by easing it out or trimming it in.

Shoal - shallow water that may be dangerous.

Shroud - standing rigging at the side of the mast.

Singlehanded - sailing alone.

S-Jibe - the controlled method of jibing with the mainsail crossing the boat under control and the boat's path makes an "S" shaped course.

Skeg - a vertical fin in front of the rudder.

Skipper - the person in charge of the boat.

Slab reefing (jiffy reefing) - lowering and tying off the lower portion of a sail in order to reduce sail area.

Slip - see **berth**.

Sloop - a single-masted sailboat with mainsail and headsail.

Snub - to hold a line under tension by wrapping it on a winch or cleat.

Sole - the floor in a cockpit or cabin.

Solenoid switch - an electrical switch which shuts off the flow of propane.

Spar - a pole used to attach a sail on a boat, for example, the mast, the boom, a gaff.

Spinnaker - a large billowing headsail used when sailing downwind.

Splice - the joining of two lines together by interweaving their strands.

Spreader - a support strut extending athwartships

from the mast used to support the mast and guide the shrouds from the top of the mast to the chainplates.

Spring line - a dockline running forward or aft from the boat to the dock to keep the boat from moving forward or aft.

Squall - a short intense storm with little warning.

Stanchions - stainless steel supports at the edge of the deck which hold the lifelines.

Standing rigging - the permanent rigging (usually wire) of a boat, including the forestay, backstay, and shrouds.

Stand-on vessel - the vessel or boat with the right-of-way.

Starboard - when looking from the stern toward the bow, the right side of the boat.

Starboard tack - sailing on any point of sail with the wind coming over the starboard side of the boat.

Stay - a wire support for a mast, part of the standing rigging.

Staysail (STAY-sil) - on a cutter, a second small "inner jib," attached between the bow and the mast.

Stem - the forward tip of the bow.

Step - the area in which the base of the mast fits.

Stern - the aft part of the boat.

Stow - to store properly.

Stuffing box (packing gland) - the opening in the hull where the propeller shaft exits.

Sump - a cavity or tank in the bilge to collect water.

Swamped - filled with water.

T

Tack - 1. - a course on which the wind comes over one side of the boat, i.e., port tack, starboard tack. 2. - to change direction by turning the bow through the wind. 3. - the lower forward corner of a sail.

Tackle - a sequence of blocks and line that provides a mechanical advantage.

Tail - to hold and pull a line from behind a winch.

Telltales - pieces of yarn or sailcloth material attached to sails which indicate when the sail is properly trimmed.

Throttle - a device for controlling the engine's revolutions per minute (RPM).

Tide - the rise and fall of water level due to the gravitational pull of the sun and moon.

Tiller - a long handle, extending into the cockpit, which directly controls the rudder.

Tiller extension - a handle attached to the tiller which allows the helmsman to sit further out to the side.

Toe rail - a short aluminum or wooden rail around the outer edges of the deck.

Toppinglift - a line used to hold the boom up when the mainsail is lowered or stowed.

Topsides - the sides of the boat between the waterline and the deck.

Transom - the vertical surface of the stern.

Traveler - a track or bridle that controls sideways (athwartships) movement of the mainsail.

Trim - 1. - to pull in on a sheet. 2. - how a sail is set relative to the wind.

Trimaran - a three-hulled sailing vessel.

True wind - the actual speed and direction of the wind when standing still.

Tune - to adjust a boat's standing rigging.

Turnbuckle - a mechanical fitting attached to the lower ends of stays, allowing for the standing rigging to be adjusted.

U

Underway - to be moving under sail or engine.

Unrig - to stow sails and rigging when the boat is not in use.

Upwind - toward the direction of the wind.

USCG - abbreviation for United States Coast Guard.

V

Vang - see **boom vang**.

Vee-berth - a bunk in the bow of the boat that narrows as it goes forward.

Veer - a clockwise change of wind direction.

Vessel - any sailboat, powerboat or ship.

VHF- abbreviation for Very High Frequency, a two-way radio commonly used for boating

W

Wake - waves caused by a boat moving through the water.

Waterline - the horizontal line on the hull of a boat where the water surface should be.

Weather helm - the boat's tendency to head up toward the wind, which occurs when a sailboat is overpowered.

Weather side - see **windward side**.

Whip - to bind together the strands at the end of a line.

Whisker pole - a pole, temporarily mounted between the mast and the clew of a jib, used to hold the jib out and keep it full when sailing downwind.

White caps - waves with foam tops.

Winch - a deck-mounted drum with a handle offering mechanical advantage used to trim sheets. Winches may also be mounted on the mast to assist in raising sails.

Windage - the amount of surface area, including sails, rigging and hull, that's presented to the wind.

Windward - toward the wind.

Windward side - the side of a boat or a sail closest to the wind.

Wing-and-wing - sailing downwind with the jib set on the opposite side of the mainsail.

Working sails - the mainsail and standard jib.

Working sheet - the leeward jib sheet that is tensioned by the wind.

Y

Yawl - a two-masted boat with its mizzen (after) mast shorter than its mainmast and located aft of the rudder post.

Y-valve - a double valve used to redirect water flow.

Phonetic Alphabet for Radio Communication

A	Alfa	N	November
B	Bravo	O	Oscar
C	Charlie	P	Pappa
D	Delta	Q	Quebec
E	Echo	R	Romeo
F	Foxtrot	S	Sierra
G	Golf	T	Tango
H	Hotel	U	Uniform
I	India	V	Victor
J	Juliet	W	Whiskey
K	Kilo	X	X-Ray
L	Lima	Y	Yankee
M	Mike	Z	Zulu

Inland Navigation Rules
NAVIGATION RULES 1-19 — INLAND

PART A — GENERAL

Rule 1 Application

(a) These Rules apply to all vessels upon the inland waters of the United States and to vessels of the United States on the Canadian waters of the Great Lakes to the extent that there is no conflict with Canadian law.

(b)(i) These Rules constitute special rules made by an appropriate authority within the meaning of Rule 1(b) of the International Regulations.

(ii) All vessels complying with the construction and equipment requirements of the International Regulations are considered to be in compliance with these Rules.

(c) Nothing in these Rules shall interfere with the operation of any special rules made by the Secretary of the Navy with respect to additional station or signal lights and shapes or whistle signals for ships of war and vessels proceeding under convoy, or by the Secretary with respect to additional station or signal lights and shapes for fishing vessels engaged in fishing as a fleet. These additional station or signal lights and shapes or whistle signals shall, so far as possible, be such that they cannot be mistaken for any light, shape, or signal authorized elsewhere under these Rules. Notice of such special rules shall be published in the Federal Register and, after the effective date specified in such notice, they shall have effect as if they were part of these Rules.

(d) Traffic separation schemes may be established for the purposes of these Rules. Vessel traffic service regulations may be in effect in certain areas.

(e) Whenever the Secretary determines that a vessel or class of vessels of special construction or purpose cannot comply fully with the provisions of any of these Rules with respect to the number, position, range, or arc of visibility of lights or shapes, as well as to the disposition and characteristics of sound-signalling appliances, the vessel shall comply with such other provisions in regard to the number, position, range, or arc of visibility of lights or shapes, as well as to the disposition and characteristics of sound-signalling appliances, as the Secretary shall have determined to be the closest possible compliance with these Rules. The Secretary may isuse a certificate of alternative compliance for a vessel or class of vessels specifying the closest possible compliance with these Rules. The Secretary of the Navy shall make these determinations and isuse certificates of alternative compliance for vessels of the Navy.

(f) The Secretary may accept a certificate of alternative compliance isused by a contracting party to the International Regulations if he determines that the alternative compliance standards of the contracting party are substantially the same as those of the United States.

Rule 2 Responsibility

(a) Nothing in these Rules shall exonerate any vessel, or the owner, master, or crew thereof, from the consequences of any neglect to comply with these Rules or of the neglect of any precaution which may be required by the ordinary practice of seamen, or by the special circumstances of the case.

(b) In construing and complying with these Rules due regard shall be had to all dangers of navigation and collision and to any special circumstances, including the limitations of the vessels involved, which may make a departure from these Rules necessary to avoid immediate danger.

Rule 3 General Definitions

For the purpose of these Rules and this Act, except where the context otherwise requires:

(a) The word "vessel" includes every description of water craft, including nondisplacement craft and seaplanes, used or capable of being used as a means of transportation on water;

(b) The term "power-driven vessel" means any vessel propelled by machinery;

(c) The term "sailing vessel" means any vessel under sail provided that propelling machinery, if fitted, is not being used;

(d) The term "vessel engaged in fishing" means any vessel fishing with nets, lines, trawls, or other fishing apparatus which restricts maneuverability, but does not include a vessel fishing with trolling lines or other fishing apparatus which do not restrict maneuverability;

(e) The word "seaplane" includes any aircraft designed to maneuver on the water;

(f) The term "vessel not under command" means a vessel which through some exceptional circumstances is unable to maneuver as required by the Rules and is therefore unable to keep out of the way of another vessel;

(g) The term "vessel restricted in her ability to maneuver" means a vessel which from the nature of her work is restricted in her ability to maneuver as required by these Rules and is therefore unable to keep out of the way of another vessel; vessels restricted in their ability to maneuver include, but are not limited to:

(i) a vessel engaged in laying, servicing, or picking up a navigation mark, submarine cable, or pipeline;

(ii) a vessel engaged in dredging, surveying, or underwater operations;

(iii) a vessel engaged in replenishment or transferring persons, provisions, or cargo while underway;

(iv) a vessel engaged in the launching or recovery of aircraft;

(v) a vessel engaged in mine clearance operations; and

(vi) a vessel engaged in a towing operation such as severely restricts the towing vessel and her tow in their ability to deviate from their course.

(h) The word "underway" means that a vessel is not at anchor, or made fast to the shore, or aground;

(i) The words "length" and "breadth" of a vessel mean her length overall and greatest breadth;

(j) Vessels shall be deemed to be in sight of one another only when one can be observed visually from the other;

(k) The term "restricted visibility" means any condition in which visibility is restricted by fog, mist, falling snow, heavy rainstorms, sandstorms, or any other similar causes;

(l) "Western Rivers" means the Mississippi River, its tributaries, South Pass, and Southwest Pass, to the navigational demarcation lines dividing the high seas from harbors, rivers, and other inland waters of the United States, and the Port Allen-Morgan City Alternate Route, and that part of the Atchafalaya River above its junction with the Port Allen-Morgan City Alternate Route including the Old River and the Red River;

(m) "Great Lakes" means the Great Lakes and their

connecting and tributary waters including the Calumet River as far as the Thomas J. O'Brien Lock and Controlling Works (between mile 326 and 327), the Chicago River as far as the east side of the Ashland Avenue Bridge (between mile 321 and 322), and the Saint Lawrence River as far east as the lower exit of Saint Lambert Lock;

(n) "Secretary" means the Secretary of the department in which the Coast Guard is operating;

(o) "Inland Waters" means the navigable waters of the United States shoreward of the navigational demarcation lines dividing the high seas from harbors, rivers, and other inland waters of the United States and the waters of the Great Lakes on the United States side of the International Boundary;

(p) "Inland Rules" or "Rules" mean the Inland Navigational Rules and the annexes thereto, which govern the conduct of vessels and specify the lights, shapes, and sound signals that apply on inland waters; and

(q) "International Regulations" means the International Regulations for Preventing Collisions at Sea, 1972, including annexes currently in force for the United States.

PART B — STEERING AND SAILING RULES

Subpart I — Conduct of Vessels in Any Condition of Visibility

Rule 4 Application
Rules in this subpart apply in any condition of visibility.

Rule 5 Look-out
Every vessel shall at all times maintain a proper look-out by sight and hearing as well as by all available means appropriate in the prevailing circumstances and conditions so as to make a full appraisal of the situation and of the risk of collision.

Rule 6 Safe Speed
Every vessel shall at all times proceed at a safe speed so that she can take proper and effective action to avoid collision and be stopped within a distance appropriate to the prevailing circumstances and conditions.

In determining a safe speed the following factors shall be among those taken into account:

(a) By all vessels:
(i) the state of visibility;
(ii) the traffic density including concentration of fishing vessels or any other vessels;
(iii) the maneuverability of the vessel with special reference to stopping distance and turning ability in the prevailing conditions;
(iv) at night the presence of background light such as from shore lights or from back scatter of her own lights;
(v) the state of wind, sea, and current, and the proximity of navigational hazards;
(vi) the draft in relation to the available depth of water.
(b) Additionally, by vessels with operational radar:
(i) the characteristics, efficiency and limitations of the radar equipment;
(ii) any constraints imposed by the radar range scale in use;
(iii) the effect on radar detection of the sea state, weather, and other sources of interference;
(iv) the possibility that small vessels, ice and other floating objects may not be detected by radar at an adequate range;
(v) the number, location, and movement of vessels detected by radar; and
(vi) the more exact assessment of the visibility that may be possible when radar is used to determine the range of vessels or other objects in the vicinity.

Rule 7 Risk of Collision
(a) Every vessel shall use all available means appropriate to the prevailing circumstances and conditions to determine if risk of collision exists. If there is any doubt such risk shall be deemed to exist.

(b) Proper use shall be made of radar equipment if fitted and operational, including long-range scanning to obtain early warning of risk of collision and radar plotting or equivalent systematic observation of detected objects.

(c) Assumptions shall not be made on the basis of scanty information, especially scanty radar information.

(d) In determining if risk of collision exists the following considerations shall be among those taken into account:
(i) such risk shall be deemed to exist if the compass bearing of an approaching vessel does not appreciably change; and
(ii) such risk may sometimes exist even when an appreciable bearing change is evident, particularly when approaching a very large vessel or a tow or when approaching a vessel at close range.

Rule 8 Action To Avoid Collision
(a) Any action taken to avoid collision shall, if the circumstances of the case admit, be positive, made in ample time and with due regard to the observance of good seamanship.

(b) Any alteration of course or speed to avoid collision shall, if the circumstances of the case admit, be large enough to be readily apparent to another vessel observing visually or by radar; a succession of small alterations of course or speed should be avoided.

(c) If there is sufficient sea room, alteration of course alone may be the most effective action to avoid a close-quarters situation provided that it is made in good time, is substantial and does not result in another close-quarters situation.

(d) Action taken to avoid collision with another vessel shall be such as to result in passing at a safe distance. The effectiveness of the action shall be carefully checked until the other vessel is finally past and clear.

(e) If necessary to avoid collision or allow more time to assess the situation, a vessel shall slacken her speed or take all way off by stopping or reversing her means of propulsion.

(f)(i) A vessel which, by any of these rules, is required not to impede the passage or safe passage of another vessel shall, when required by the circumstances of the case, take early action to allow sufficient sea room for the safe passage of the other vessel.

(ii) A vessel required not to impede the passage or safe passage of another vessel is not relieved of this obligation if approaching the other vessel so as to involve risk of collision and shall, when taking action, have full regard to the action which may be required by the rules of this part.

(iii) A vessel, the passage of which is not to be impeded remains fully obliged to comply with the rules of this part when the two vessels are approaching one another so as to involve risk of collision.

Rule 9 Narrow Channels

(a)(i) A vessel proceeding along the course of a narrow channel or fairway shall keep as near to the outer limit of the channel or fairway which lies on her starboard side as is safe and practicable.

(ii) Notwithstanding paragraph (a)(i) and Rule 14(a), a power-driven vessel operating in narrow channels or fairways on the Great Lakes, Western Rivers, or waters specified by the Secretary, and proceeding downbound with a following current shall have the right-of-way over an upbound vessel, shall propose the manner and place of passage, and shall initiate the maneuvering signals prescribed by Rule 34(a)(i), as appropriate. The vessel proceeding upbound against the current shall hold as necessary to permit safe passing.

(b) A vessel of less than 20 meters in length or a sailing vessel shall not impede the passage of a vessel that can safely navigate only within a narrow channel or fairway.

(c) A vessel engaged in fishing shall not impede the passage of any other vessel navigating within a narrow channel or fairway.

(d) A vessel shall not cross a narrow channel or fairway if such crossing impedes the passage of a vessel which can safely navigate only within that channel or fairway. The latter vessel shall use the danger signal prescribed in Rule 34(d) if in doubt as to the intention of the crossing vessel.

(e)(i) In a narrow channel or fairway when overtaking, the vessel intending to overtake shall indicate her intention by sounding the appropriate signal prescribed in Rule 34(c) and take steps to permit safe passing. The overtaken vessel, if in agreement, shall sound the same signal. If in doubt she shall sound the danger signal prescribed in Rule 34(d).

(ii) This Rule does not relieve the overtaking vessel of her obligation under Rule 13.

(f) A vessel nearing a bend or an area of a narrow channel or fairway where other vessels may be obscured by an intervening obstruction shall navigate with particular alertness and caution and shall sound the appropriate signal prescribed in Rule 34(e).

(g) Every vessel shall, if the circumstances of the case admit, avoid anchoring in a narrow channel.

Rule 10 Traffic Separation Schemes

(a) This Rule applies to traffic separation schemes and does not relieve any vessel of her obligation under any other rule.

(b) A vessel using a traffic separation scheme shall:

(i) proceed in the appropriate traffic lane in the general direction of traffic flow for that lane;

(ii) so far as practicable keep clear of a traffic separation line or separation zone;

(iii) normally join or leave a traffic lane at the termination of the lane, but when joining or leaving from either side shall do so at as small an angle to the general direction of traffic flow as practicable.

(c) A vessel shall, so far as practicable, avoid crossing traffic lanes but if obliged to do so shall cross on a heading as nearly as practicable at right angles to the general direction of traffic flow.

(d)(i) A vessel shall not use an inshore traffic zone when she can safely use the appropriate traffic lane within the adjacent traffic separation scheme. However, vessels of less than 20 meters in length, sailing vessels and vessels engaged in fishing may use the inshore traffic zone.

(ii) Notwithstanding sub-paragraph (d)(i), a vessel may use an inshore traffic zone when en route to or from a port, offshore installation or structure, pilot station or any other place situated within the inshore traffic zone, or to avoid immediate danger.

(e) A vessel other than a crossing vessel or a vessel joining or leaving a lane shall not normally enter a separation zone or cross a separation line except:

(i) in cases of emergency to avoid immediate danger;

(ii) to engage in fishing within a separation zone.

(f) A vessel navigating in areas near the terminations of traffic separation schemes shall do so with particular caution.

(g) A vessel shall so far as practicable avoid anchoring in a traffic separation scheme or in areas near its terminations.

(h) A vessel not using a traffic separation scheme shall avoid it by as wide a margin as is practicable.

(i) A vessel engaged in fishing shall not impede the passage of any vessel following a traffic lane.

(j) A vessel of less than 20 meters in length or a sailing vessel shall not impede the safe passage of a power-driven vessel following a traffic lane.

(k) A vessel restricted in her ability to maneuver when engaged in an operation for the maintenance of safety of navigation in a traffic separation scheme is exempted from complying with this Rule to the extent necessary to carry out the operation.

(l) A vessel restricted in her ability to maneuver when engaged in an operation for the laying, servicing or picking up of a submarine cable, within a traffic separation scheme, is exempted from complying with this Rule to the extent necessary to carry out the operation.

Subpart II — Conduct of Vessels in Sight of One Another

Rule 11 Application

Rules in this subpart apply to vessels in sight of one another.

Rule 12 Sailing Vessels

(a) When two sailing vessels are approaching one another, so as to involve risk of collision, one of them shall keep out of the way of the other as follows:

(i) when each has the wind on a different side, the vessel which has the wind on the port side shall keep out of the way of the other;

(ii) when both have the wind on the same side, the vessel which is to windward shall keep out of the way of the vessel which is to leeward; and

(iii) if a vessel with the wind on the port side sees a vessel to windward and cannot determine with certainty whether the other vessel has the wind on the port or on the starboard side, she shall keep out of the way of the other.

(b) For the purpose of this Rule the windward side shall be deemed to be the side opposite to that on which the mainsail is carried or, in the case of a square-rigged vessel, the side opposite to that on which the largest fore-and-aft sail is carried.

Rule 13 Overtaking

(a) Notwithstanding anything contained in Rules 4 through 18, any vessel overtaking any other shall keep out of the way of the vessel being overtaken.

(b) A vessel shall be deemed to be overtaking when coming up with another vessel from a direction more than 22.5

degrees abaft her beam; that is, in such a position with reference to the vessel she is overtaking, that at night she would be able to see only the sternlight of that vessel but neither of her sidelights.

(c) When a vessel is in any doubt as to whether she is overtaking another, she shall assume that this is the case and act accordingly.

(d) Any subsequent alteration of the bearing between the two vessels shall not make the overtaking vessel a crossing vessel within the meaning of these Rules or relieve her of the duty of keeping clear of the overtaken vessel until she is finally past and clear.

Rule 14 Head-on Situation

(a) Unless otherwise agreed, when two power-driven vessels are meeting on reciprocal or nearly reciprocal courses so as to involve risk of collision each shall alter her course to starboard so that each shall pass on the port side of the other.

(b) Such a situation shall be deemed to exist when a vessel sees the other ahead or nearly ahead and by night she could see the masthead lights of the other in a line or nearly in a line or both sidelights and by day she observes the corresponding aspect of the other vessel.

(c) When a vessel is in any doubt as to whether such a situation exists she shall assume that it does exist and act accordingly.

(d) Notwithstanding paragraph (a) of this Rule, a power-driven vessel operating on the Great Lakes, Western Rivers, or waters specified by the Secretary, and proceeding downbound with a following current shall have the right-of-way over an upbound vessel, shall propose the manner of passage, and shall initiate the maneuvering signals prescribed by Rule 34(a)(i), as appropriate.

Rule 15 Crossing Situation

(a) When two power-driven vessels are crossing so as to involve risk of collision, the vessel which has the other on her starboard side shall keep out of the way and shall, if the circumstances of the case admit, avoid crossing ahead of the other vessel.

(b) Notwithstanding paragraph (a), on the Great Lakes, Western Rivers, or water specified by the Secretary, a vessel crossing a river shall keep out of the way of a power-driven vessel ascending or descending the river.

Rule 16 Action by Give-Way Vessel

Every vessel which is directed to keep out of the way of another vessel shall, so far as possible, take early and substantial action to keep well clear.

Rule 17 Action by Stand-on Vessel

(a)(i) Where one of two vessels is to keep out of the way, the other shall keep her course and speed.

(ii) The latter vessel may, however, take action to avoid collision by her maneuver alone, as soon as it becomes apparent to her that the vessel required to keep out of the way is not taking appropriate action in compliance with these Rules.

(b) When, from any cause, the vessel required to keep her course and speed finds herself so close that collision cannot be avoided by the action of the give-way vessel alone, she shall take such action as will best aid to avoid collision.

(c) A power-driven vessel which takes action in a crossing situation in accordance with subparagraph (a)(ii) of this Rule to avoid collision with another power-driven vessel shall, if the circumstances of the case admit, not alter course to port for a vessel on her own port side.

(d) This Rule does not relieve the give-way vessel of her obligation to keep out of the way.

Rule 18 Responsibilities Between Vessels

Except where Rules 9, 10, and 13 otherwise require:

(a) A power-driven vessel underway shall keep out of the way of:
(i) a vessel not under command;
(ii) a vessel restricted in her ability to maneuver;
(iii) a vessel engaged in fishing; and
(iv) a sailing vessel.

(b) A sailing vessel underway shall keep out of the way of:
(i) a vessel not under command;
(ii) a vessel restricted in her ability to maneuver; and
(iii) a vessel engaged in fishing.

(c) A vessel engaged in fishing when underway shall, so far as possible, keep out of the way of:
(i) a vessel not under command; and
(ii) a vessel restricted in her ability to maneuver.

(d) A seaplane on the water shall, in general, keep well clear of all vessels and avoid impeding their navigation. In circumstances, however, where risk of collision exists, she shall comply with the Rules of this Part.

Subpart III — Conduct of Vessels in Restricted Visibility

Rule 19 Conduct of Vessels in Restricted Visibility

(a) This Rule applies to vessels not in sight of one another when navigating in or near an area of restricted visibility.

(b) Every vessel shall proceed at a safe speed adapted to the prevailing circumstances and conditions of restricted visibility. A power-driven vessel shall have her engines ready for immediate maneuver.

(c) Every vessel shall have due regard to the prevailing circumstances and conditions of restricted visibility when complying with Rules 4 through 10.

(d) A vessel which detects by radar alone the presence of another vessel shall determine if a close-quarters situation is developing or risk of collision exists. If so, she shall take avoiding action in ample time, provided that when such action consists of an alteration of course, so far as possible the following shall be avoided:
(i) an alteration of course to port for a vessel forward of the beam, other than for a vessel being overtaken; and
(ii) an alteration of course toward a vessel abeam or abaft the beam.

(e) Except where it has been determined that a risk of collision does not exist, every vessel which hears apparently forward of her beam the fog signal of another vessel, or which cannot avoid a close-quarters situation with another vessel forward of her beam, shall reduce her speed to the minimum at which she can be kept on course. She shall if necessary take all her way off and, in any event, navigate with extreme caution until danger of collision is over.

International Navigation Rules

NAVIGATION RULES 1-19 — INTERNATIONAL

PART A — GENERAL

Rule 1 Application
(a) These Rules shall apply to all vessels upon the high seas and in all waters connected therewith navigable by seagoing vessels.

(b) Nothing in these Rules shall interfere with the operation of special rules made by an appropriate authority for roadsteads, harbors, rivers, lakes or inland waterways connected with the high seas and navigable by seagoing vessels. Such special rules shall conform as closely as possible to these rules.

(c) Nothing in these Rules shall interfere with the operation of special rules made by the Government of any State with respect to additional station or signal lights, shapes or whistle signals for ships of war and vessels proceeding under convoy, or with respect to additional station or signal lights or shapes for fishing vessels engaged in fishing as a fleet. These additional station or signal lights, shapes or whistle signals shall, so far as possible, be such that they cannot be mistaken for any light, shape or signal authorized elsewhere under these Rules.

(d) Traffic separation schemes may be adopted by the Organization for the purpose of these Rules.

(e) Whenever the Government concerned shall have determined that a vessel of special construction or purpose cannot comply fully with the provisions of any of these Rules with respect to the number, position, range or arc of visibility of lights or shapes, as well as to the disposition and characteristics of sound-signalling appliances, such vessel shall comply with such other provisions in regard to the number, position, range or arc of visibility of lights or shapes, as well as to the disposition and characteristics of sound-signalling appliances, as her Government shall have determined to be the closest possible compliance with these Rules in respect of that vessel.

Rule 2 Responsibility
(a) Nothing in these Rules shall exonerate any vessel, or the owner, master or crew thereof, from the consequences of any neglect to comply with these Rules or of the neglect of any precaution which may be required by the ordinary practice of seamen, or by the special circumstances of the case.

(b) In construing and complying with these Rules due regard shall be had to all dangers of navigation and collision and to any special circumstances, including the limitations of the vessels involved, which may make a departure from these Rules necessary to avoid immediate danger.

Rule 3 General Definitions
For the purpose of these Rules, except where the context otherwise requires:

(a) The word "vessel" includes every description of water craft, including nondisplacement craft and seaplanes, used or capable of being used as a means of transportation on water.

(b) The term "power-driven vessel" means any vessel propelled by machinery.

(c) The term "sailing vessel" means any vessel under sail provided that propelling machinery, if fitted, is not being used.

(d) The term "vessel engaged in fishing" means any vessel fishing with nets, lines, trawls or other fishing apparatus which restrict maneuverability, but does not include a vessel fishing with trolling lines or other fishing apparatus which do not restrict maneuverability.

(e) The word "seaplane" includes any aircraft designed to maneuver on the water.

(f) The term "vessel not under command" means a vessel which through some exceptional circumstance is unable to maneuver as required by these Rules and is therefore unable to keep out of the way of another vessel.

(g) The term "vessel restricted in her ability to maneuver" means a vessel which from the nature of her work is restricted in her ability to maneuver as required by these Rules and is therefore unable to keep out of the way of another vessel.

The term "vessels restricted in their ability to maneuver" shall include but not be limited to:

(i) a vessel engaged in laying, servicing or picking up a navigation mark, submarine cable or pipeline;

(ii) a vessel engaged in dredging, surveying or underwater operations;

(iii) a vessel engaged in replenishment or transferring persons, provisions or cargo while underway;

(iv) a vessel engaged in the launching or recovery of aircraft;

(v) a vessel engaged in mine clearance operations;

(vi) a vessel engaged in a towing operation such as severely restricts the towing vessel and her tow in their ability to deviate from their course.

(h) The term "vessel constrained by her draft" means a power-driven vessel which, because of her draft in relation to the available depth and width of navigable water is severely restricted in her ability to deviate from the course she is following.

(i) The word "underway" means that a vessel is not at anchor, or made fast to the shore, or aground.

(j) The words "length" and "breadth" of a vessel mean her length overall and greatest breadth.

(k) Vessels shall be deemed to be in sight of one another only when one can be observed visually from the other.

(l) The term "restricted visibility" means any condition in which visibility is restricted by fog, mist, falling snow, heavy rainstorms, sandstorms or any other similar causes.

PART B — STEERING AND SAILING RULES
Section I — Conduct of Vessels in Any Condition of Visibility

Rule 4 Application
Rules in this Section apply to any condition of visibility.

Rule 5 Look-out
Every vessel shall at all times maintain a proper look-out by sight and hearing as well as by all available means appropriate in the prevailing circumstances and conditions so

as to make a full appraisal of the situation and of the risk of collision.

Rule 6 Safe Speed

Every vessel shall at all times proceed at a safe speed so that she can take proper and effective action to avoid collision and be stopped within a distance appropriate to the prevailing circumstances and conditions.

In determining a safe speed the following factors shall be among those taken into account:

(a) By all vessels:

(i) the state of visibility;

(ii) the traffic density including concentrations of fishing vessels or any other vessels;

(iii) the maneuverability of the vessel with special reference to stopping distance and turning ability in the prevailing conditions;

(iv) at night the presence of background light such as from shore lights or from back scatter of her own lights;

(v) the state of wind, sea and current, and the proximity of navigational hazards;

(vi) the draft in relation to the available depth of water.

(b) Additionally, by vessels with operational radar:

(i) the characteristics, efficiency and limitations of the radar equipment;

(ii) any constraints imposed by the radar range scale in use;

(iii) the effect on radar detection of the sea state, weather and other sources of interference;

(iv) the possibility that small vessels, ice and other floating objects may not be detected by radar at an adequate range;

(v) the number, location, and movement of vessels detected by radar.

(vi) the more exact assessment of the visibility that may be possible when radar is used to determine the range of vessels or other objects in the vicinity.

Rule 7 Risk of Collision

(a) Every vessel shall use all available means appropriate to the prevailing circumstances and conditions to determine if risk of collision exists. If there is any doubt such risk shall be deemed to exist.

(b) Proper use shall be made of radar equipment if fitted and operational, including long-range scanning to obtain early warning of risk of collision and radar plotting or equivalent systematic observation of detected objects.

(c) Assumptions shall not be made on the basis of scanty information, especially scanty radar information.

(d) In determining if risk of collision exists the following considerations shall be among those taken into account:

(i) such risk shall be deemed to exist if the compass bearing of an approaching vessel does not appreciably change;

(ii) such risk may sometimes exist even when an appreciable bearing change is evident, particularly when approaching a very large vessel or a tow or when approaching a vessel at close range.

Rule 8 Action To Avoid Collision

(a) Any action taken to avoid collision shall, if the circumstances of the case admit, be positive, made in ample time and with due regard to the observance of good seamanship.

(b) Any alteration of course and/or speed to avoid collision shall, if the circumstances of the case admit, be large enough to be readily apparent to another vessel observing visually or by radar; a succession of small alterations of course and/or speed should be avoided.

(c) If there is sufficient sea room, alteration of course alone may be the most effective action to avoid a close-quarters situation provided that it is made in good time, is substantial and does not result in another close-quarters situation.

(d) Action taken to avoid collision with another vessel shall be such as to result in passing at a safe distance. The effectiveness of the action shall be carefully checked until the other vessel is finally past and clear.

(e) If necessary to avoid collision or allow more time to assess the situation, a vessel shall slacken her speed to take all way off by stopping or reversing her means of propulsion.

(f)(i) A vessel which, by any of these rules, is required not to impede the passage or safe passage of another vessel shall, when required by the circumstances of the case, take early action to allow sufficient sea room for the safe passage of the other vessel.

(ii) A vessel required not to impede the passage or safe passage of another vessel is not relieved of this obligation if approaching the other vessel so as to involve risk of collision and shall, when taking action, have full regard to the action which may be required by the rules of this part.

(iii) A vessel, the passage of which is not to be impeded remains fully obliged to comply with the rules of this part when the two vessels are approaching one another so as to involve risk of collision.

Rule 9 Narrow Channels

a) A vessel proceeding along the course of a narrow channel or fairway shall keep as near to the outer limit of the channel or fairway which lies on her starboard side as is safe and practicable.

(b) A vessel of less than 20 meters in length or a sailing vessel shall not impede the passage of a vessel which can safely navigate only within a narrow channel or fairway.

(c) A vessel engaged in fishing shall not impede the passage of any other vessel navigating within a narrow channel or fairway.

(d) A vessel shall not cross a narrow channel or fairway if such crossing impedes the passage of a vessel which can safely navigate only within such channel or fairway. The latter vessel may use the sound signal prescribed in Rule 34(d) if in doubt as to the intention of the crossing vessel.

(e)(i) In a narrow channel or fairway when overtaking can take place only if the vessel to be overtaken has to take action to permit safe passing, the vessel intending to overtake shall indicate her intention by sounding the appropriate signal prescribed in Rule 34(c)(i). The vessel to be overtaken shall, if in agreement, sound the appropriate signal prescribed in Rule 34(c)(ii) and take steps to permit safe passing. If in doubt she may sound the signal prescribed in Rule 34(d).

(ii) This Rule does not relieve the overtaking vessel of her obligation under Rule 13.

(f) A vessel nearing a bend or an area of a narrow channel or fairway where other vessels may be obscured by an intervening obstruction shall navigate with particular alertness and caution and shall sound the appropriate signal prescribed in Rule 34(e).

(g) Any vessel shall, if the circumstances of the case admit, avoid anchoring in a narrow channel.

Rule 10 Traffic Separation Schemes

(a) This Rule applies to traffic separation schemes adopted by the Organization and does not relieve any vessel of her obligation under any other rule.

(b) A vessel using a traffic separation scheme shall:

(i) proceed in the appropriate traffic lane in the general direction of traffic flow for that lane;

(ii) so far as practicable keep clear of a traffic separation line or separation zone;

(iii) normally join or leave a traffic lane at the termination of the lane, but when joining or leaving from either side shall do so at as small an angle to the general direction of traffic flow as practicable.

(c) A vessel shall, so far as practicable, avoid crossing traffic lanes but if obliged to do so shall cross on a heading as nearly as practicable at right angles to the general direction of traffic flow.

(d)(i) A vessel shall not use an inshore traffic zone when she can safely use the appropriate traffic lane within the adjacent traffic separation scheme. However, vessels of less than 20 meters in length, sailing vessels and vessels engaged in fishing may use the inshore traffic zone.

(ii) Notwithstanding subparagraph (d)(i), a vessel may use an inshore traffic zone when en route to or from a port, offshore installation or structure, pilot station or any other place situated within the inshore traffic zone, or to avoid immediate danger.

(e) A vessel other than a crossing vessel or a vessel joining or leaving a lane shall not normally enter a separation zone or cross a separation line except:

(i) in cases of emergency to avoid immediate danger;

(ii) to engage in fishing within a separation zone.

(f) A vessel navigating in areas near the terminations of traffic separation schemes shall do so with particular caution.

(g) A vessel shall so far as practicable avoid anchoring in a traffic separation scheme or in areas near its terminations.

(h) A vessel not using a traffic separation scheme shall avoid it by as wide a margin as is practicable.

(i) A vessel engaged in fishing shall not impede the passage of any vessel following a traffic lane.

(j) A vessel of less than 20 meters in length or a sailing vessel shall not impede the safe passage of a power-driven vessel following a traffic lane.

(k) A vessel restricted in her ability to maneuver when engaged in an operation for the maintenance of safety of navigation in a traffic separation scheme is exempted from complying with this Rule to the extent necessary to carry out the operation.

(l) A vessel restricted in her ability to maneuver when engaged in an operation for the laying, servicing or picking up of a submarine cable, within a traffic separation scheme, is exempted from complying with this Rule to the extent necessary to carry out the operation.

Section II — Conduct of Vessels in Sight of One Another

Rule 11 Application

Rules in this Section apply to vessels in sight of one another.

Rule 12 Sailing Vessels

(a) When two sailing vessels are approaching one another, so as to involve risk of collision, one of them shall keep out of the way of the other as follows:

(i) when each has the wind on a different side, the vessel which has the wind on the port side shall keep out of the way of the other;

(ii) when both have the wind on the same side, the vessel which is to windward shall keep out of the way of the vessel which is to leeward;

(iii) if a vessel with the wind on the port side sees a vessel to windward and cannot determine with certainty whether the other vessel has the wind on the port or on the starboard side, she shall keep out of the way of the other.

(b) For the purposes of this Rule the windward side shall be deemed to be the side opposite to that on which the mainsail is carried or, in the case of a square-rigged vessel, the side opposite to that on which the largest fore-and-aft sail is carried.

Rule 13 Overtaking

(a) Notwithstanding anything contained in the Rules of Part B, Sections I and II any vessel overtaking any other shall keep out of the way of the vessel being overtaken.

(b) A vessel shall be deemed to be overtaking when coming up with another vessel from a direction more than 22.5 degrees abaft her beam, that is, in such a position with reference to the vessel she is overtaking, that at night she would be able to see only the sternlight of that vessel but neither of her sidelights.

(c) When a vessel is in any doubt as to whether she is overtaking another, she shall assume that this is the case and act accordingly.

(d) Any subsequent alteration of the bearing between the two vessels shall not make the overtaking vessel a crossing vessel within the meaning of these Rules or relieve her of the duty of keeping clear of the overtaken vessel until she is finally past and clear.

Rule 14 Head-on Situation

(a) When two power-driven vessels are meeting on reciprocal or nearly reciprocal courses so as to involve risk of collision each shall alter her course to starboard so that each shall pass on the port side of the other.

(b) Such a situation shall be deemed to exist when a vessel sees the other ahead or nearly ahead and by night she could see the masthead lights of the other in a line or nearly in a line and/or both sidelights and by day she observes the corresponding aspect of the other vessel.

(c) When a vessel is in any doubt as to whether such a situation exists she shall assume that it does exist and act accordingly.

Rule 15 Crossing Situation

When two power-driven vessels are crossing so as to involve risk of collision, the vessel which has the other on her own starboard side shall keep out of the way and shall, if the circumstances of the case admit, avoid crossing ahead of the other vessel.

Rule 16 Action by Give-way Vessel

Every vessel which is directed to keep out of the way of another vessel shall, so far as possible, take early and substantial action to keep well clear.

Rule 17 Action by Stand-on Vessel

(a)(i) Where one of two vessels is to keep out of the way the other shall keep her course and speed.

(ii) The latter vessel may however take action to avoid collision by her maneuver alone, as soon as it becomes apparent to her that the vessel required to keep out of the way is not taking appropriate action in compliance with these Rules.

(b) When, from any cause, the vessel required to keep her course and speed finds herself so close that collision cannot be avoided by the action of the give-way vessel alone, she shall take such action as will best aid to avoid collision.

(c) A power-driven vessel which takes action in a crossing situation in accordance with subparagraph (a)(ii) of this Rule to avoid collision with another power-driven vessel shall, if the circumstances of the case admit, not alter course to port for a vessel on her own port side.

(d) This Rule does not relieve the give-way vessel of her obligation to keep out of the way.

Rule 18 Responsibilities between Vessels
Except where Rules 9, 10 and 13 otherwise require:

(a) A power-driven vessel underway shall keep out of the way of:
(i) a vessel not under command;
(ii) a vessel restricted in her ability to maneuver;
(iii) a vessel engaged in fishing;
(iv) a sailing vessel.

(b) A sailing vessel underway shall keep out of the way of:
(i) a vessel not under command;
(ii) a vessel restricted in her ability to maneuver;
(iii) a vessel engaged in fishing.

(c) A vessel engaged in fishing when underway shall, so far as possible, keep out of the way of:
(i) a vessel not under command;
(ii) a vessel restricted in her ability to maneuver.

(d)(i) Any vessel other than a vessel not under command or a vessel restricted in her ability to maneuver shall, if the circumstances of the case admit, avoid impeding the safe passage of a vessel constrained by her draft, exhibiting the signals in Rule 28.

(ii) A vessel constrained by her draft shall navigate with particular caution having full regard to her special condition.

(e) A seaplane on the water shall, in general, keep well clear of all vessels and avoid impeding their navigation. In circumstances, however, where risk of collision exists, she shall comply with the Rules of this Part.

Section III — Conduct of Vessels in Restricted Visibility

Rule 19 Conduct of Vessels in Restricted Visibility
(a) This Rule applies to vessels not in sight of one another when navigating in or near an area of restricted visibility.

(b) Every vessel shall proceed at a safe speed adapted to the prevailing circumstances and conditions of restricted visibility. A power-driven vessel shall have her engines ready for immediate maneuver.

(c) Every vessel shall have due regard to the prevailing circumstances and conditions of restricted visibility when complying with the Rules of Section I of this Part.

(d) A vessel which detects by radar alone the presence of another vessel shall determine if a close-quarters situation is developing and/or risk of collision exists. If so, she shall take avoiding action in ample time, provided that when such action consists of an alteration of course, so far as possible the following shall be avoided:
(i) an alteration of course to port for a vessel forward of the beam, other than for a vessel being overtaken;
(ii) an alteration of course toward a vessel abeam or abaft the beam.

(e) Except where it has been determined that a risk of collision does not exist, every vessel which hears apparently forward of her beam the fog signal of another vessel, or which cannot avoid a close-quarters situation with another vessel forward of her beam, shall reduce her speed to the minimum at which she can be kept on her course. She shall if necessary take all her way off and in any event navigate with extreme caution until danger of collision is over.

A complete set of the Navigation Rules, International-Inland (COMDTINST M16672.2B) is available at most marine bookstores, chandleries or the U.S. Government Printing Office (202-783-3238).

US SAILING Basic Cruising Certification

To responsibly skipper and crew an auxiliary pow-
ered cruising sailboat during daylight hours within
sight of land in moderate wind and sea conditions.

Recommended Equipment: It is recommended
that Basic Cruising Certification courses and
examinations be conducted on 23' to 35' sloop-
rigged cruising keelboats with auxiliary power and
with adequate equipment inventory to complete
all required certification outcomes.

Prerequisite: The prerequisite for Basic Cruising
Certification is Basic Keelboat Certification or suc-
cessful completion of a Basic Keelboat
Certification equivalency examination.

Certification Requirements: Basic Cruising
Certification requires the successful completion of
the following knowledge and skill requirements.
These requirements are expected to be performed
safely with confident command of the boat in a
wind range of 5 to 15 knots. Some regions may
have stronger prevailing conditions, which are
acceptable if the candidate can safely control the
boat, and be aware of his or her limitations in
these conditions. The certified candidate will be
able to skipper a keelboat up to 30 feet in length.

Part 1: Minimum Water Skills

Preparation to Sail:
1. Demonstrate ability to recognize and fore-
cast prevailing local weather conditions.
2. Perform an inspection of running rigging,
standing rigging and hull integrity.
3. Check the inventory, location and operation
of required safety equipment.
4. Check the auxiliary power systems: location
and operation of engine controls, engine
mechanical and fluids check, transmission
controls, ventilation system and cooling
system.
5. Check the electrical system: main battery
switch, electrical control panel, battery
fluids and battery terminals.
6. Check the bilge pump system: operation of

manual and electrical pumps, intake maintenance and bilge pump alarms.
7. Check the head systems: location of controls, equipment operation, holding tanks,
and proper setting of valves.
8. Check the fresh water system: adequate
quantity, operation of manual and electrical
pumps, and proper setting of valves.
9. Check the anchoring system: anchors,
shackles, rodes, chafing equipment, and
windlass.
10. Check all other equipment specific to your
boat not indicated above.

Crew Operations and Skills:
11. Demonstrate winch operation and
procedure for clearing a fouled winch.
12. Demonstrate tying and use of knots: clove
hitch, two half-hitches, sheet bend and
rolling hitch. Review stopper knot, bowline,
cleat hitch and sail lashing knot.
13. Demonstrate how to heave a line.
14. Demonstrate the use of sail controls: hal
yards, sheets, traveler, cunningham/down
haul, outhaul, adjustable backstay (if appli-
cable), boom vang, leech lines, jib fairleads
and boom toppinglift.
15. Demonstrate the operation of a VHF radio:
operation of controls, channel usage, call
sign, weather channels, and simulate an
emergency call.

Leaving the Dock or Mooring:
16. Demonstrate appropriate helmsman and
crew coordination and skills for departure
under power suitable to the conditions: line
handling, casting off, fending off, and
boathandling.
17. Demonstrate the use of docklines for boat
control while departing.
18. Demonstrate stowing of docklines and
fenders.

Boat Control in Confined Waters:
19. Demonstrate in close quarters under power:
speed and momentum control, windage and
prop walk control, and command of the
crew.
20. Demonstrate ability to maneuver under sail
in close quarters: short tacking and
controlled jibes.
21. Demonstrate a recovery plan for an engine
failure in a crowded and busy harbor.

Navigation (Piloting):

22. Demonstrate ability to identify chart symbols and corresponding visual observations.
23. Demonstrate basic dead reckoning: plotting course and position, calculating time/speed/distance, taking bearings and fixes, and plotting danger bearings.

Boat Control in Open Water:

24. Demonstrate ability to steer a compass course with changes in course to a given destination.
25. Demonstrate helm and boat control in a variety of wind and sea conditions.

Heavy Weather Sailing:

26. Demonstrate proper reefing techniques: determining when to reef, roller furling or changing headsails, reefing the mainsail, dropping sails, shaking out a reef, and rehoisting underway.
27. Demonstrate helm and boat control while sailing under shortened sail.

Overboard Recovery Methods:

28. Properly demonstrate one of the overboard recovery methods, which is most appropriate for: your sailing ability, boat type, crew experience, wind and sea conditions, and maintaining constant visual contact with the victim.

Safety and Emergency Procedures:

29. Simulate procedure and operation of VHF radio in various emergency situations.
30. Simulate failure of steering system, and demonstrate steering and boat control with sails.

Anchoring Techniques:

31. Select an anchorage, and demonstrate appropriate helmsman and crew coordination and skills for properly anchoring with a single anchor under power.
32. Demonstrate appropriate helmsman and crew coordination and skills for retrieving your anchor under power.

Returning to the Dock or Mooring:

33. Demonstrate appropriate helmsman and crew coordination and skills for arrival under power suitable to the conditions: boathandling, deploying fenders, stopping and tying up.
34. Demonstrate appropriate helmsman and

crew coordination and skills for arrival under sail suitable to the conditions: boathandling, deploying fenders, stopping and tying up.

Securing the Boat Properly:

35. Demonstrate stowing of sails, rigging and equipment. Thoroughly clean the boat, and install any covers and dock power equipment.
36. Check both the electrical and bilge systems for dock operation.
37. Check the locks on companionway, lockers and hatches. Make a final check of docklines, spring lines and fender placement.

Part 2: Minimum Knowledge

Crew Operations and Skills:

1. Describe typical crew responsibilities and communications while aboard an auxiliary powered cruising sailboat.
2. Explain weather recognition and forecasting techniques for a two to three day period.
3. Explain the sequence for determining blocked engine cooling system circulation.
4. Understand the different types and operation of stoves, and fuel systems.
5. Be familiar with the use of a float plan.

Sailing Theory:

6. Describe sailboat dynamics: Center of Effort, Center of Lateral Resistance, and effects and influences of Lee and Weather Helm.
7. Describe real and apparent wind, and their relationship to each other.

Leaving the Dock or Mooring:

8. Understand the effects of wind, tide and currents in relation to the boat and surrounding area, while preparing to get underway.
9. Describe the differences and alternatives for leaving under power in upwind, crosswind and downwind situations.

Navigation (Piloting):

10. Be familiar with magnetic influences that may disrupt compass readings.
11. Define true and magnetic compass readings and application of variation and deviation.

Navigation Rules, International-Inland:

12. Know the Navigation Rules, International-Inland, Rules 4 through 10 for steering and

sailing.

13. Know how to access the Navigation Rules, International-Inland, Rules 20 through 31 to identify and use dayshapes, and Rules 32 through 38 to identify and use sound signals.

Boat Control in Open Water:

14. Explain the advantages of "working to weather" and in gaining an upwind advantage.

Overboard Recovery Methods:

15. Understand the Quick-Stop, Lifesling-type, and Quick-Turn overboard recovery methods under sail to include: constant visual contact with the victim, communications, recovery plan, sequence of maneuvers, boathandling, course sailed, pickup approach, coming alongside the victim (or simulated object), and bringing the victim aboard.

16. Explain when overboard recovery should be done under power and the inherent dangers.

Safety and Emergency Procedures:

17. Describe recovery methods after going aground.

18. Be familiar with fire fighting equipment on board: regulations, types, location and operation.

19. Be familiar with the location and operation of emergency steering system and boat control during failure of the steering system.

20. Understand towing techniques: maneuvering onto a tow, handling and securing a towline, chafing protection, boat speed, dropping off a tow, and communications.

21. Describe the function of lifelines and pulpits.

22. Explain proper fueling techniques and potential hazards.

23. Explain the purpose and use of a radar reflector.

24. Be familiar with U.S. Coast Guard safety requirements for auxiliary powered vessels.

25. Be familiar with at least six distress or emergency signals.

26. Explain the proper procedures for protection against lightning strikes.

Anchoring Techniques:

27. Explain different types of anchors and various bottom conditions suited for each type.

28. Explain how to determine the required scope of an anchor rode.

29. Describe accepted etiquette when anchoring in the vicinity of other boats.

Returning to the Dock or Mooring:

30. Describe the differences and alternatives for docking under power in upwind, crosswind, and downwind situations.

An introduction to US SAILING.

Since 1897 the United States Sailing Association (US SAILING) has provided support for American sailors at all levels of sailing — in all kinds of sailboats. The primary objective of its Training Program is to provide a national standard of quality instruction for all people learning to sail. The US SAILING Keelboat Certification System includes a series of books such as *Basic Cruising*, a program of student certifications and an extensive educational and training program for instructors. It is one of the most highly developed and effective national training systems for students and sailing instructors and is recognized nationally and internationally.

US SAILING is a non-profit organization and the official National Governing Body of Sailing as designated by the U. S. Congress in the Amateur Sports Act. It has a national Training Program for sailors in dinghies, windsurfers, multihulls and keelboats. It is also the official representative to the International Yacht Racing Union (IYRU).

The US SAILING Keelboat Certification System is designed to develop safe, responsible and confident sailors who meet specific performance and knowledge standards. (See US SAILING BASIC CRUISING Certification on page 122 for the BASIC CRUISING standards.) There are other benefits for you as well. You can start at the BASIC KEELBOAT certification level and progress through BASIC CRUISING, BAREBOAT CRUISING, COASTAL NAVIGATION, and even go on to COASTAL PASSAGE MAKING, CELESTIAL NAVIGATION and OFFSHORE PASSAGE

MAKING. With your US SAILING certifications and experience documented in the *Official Logbook of Sailing*, you will have a passport to cruising and chartering boats locally or worldwide.

Basic Cruising is intended as a supplement to your sailing lessons, rather than as a substitute for them. It was created to help you accelerate your learning curve and clarify your understanding of the concepts and techniques of sailing and cruising.

What Makes Sailing Special?

Within the past 20 years, the advent of fiberglass boatbuilding and other new technologies has opened up the sport of sailing to people of all ages, incomes and abilities. Sailing offers virtually limitless choices of boats, each with its own unique characteristics, and the opportunity to explore an adjacent cove or an exotic tropical location.

Most sailors will acquire entry-level skills quite rapidly. However, mastering them is an experience that will be rewarding, exciting and pleasurable for a lifetime.

As you continue to sail, you will find that sailing is more than simply being pushed and pulled by the wind. For most people, sailing is meeting new friends, enjoying nature's beauty and challenge, and sharing a unique fellowship with all boaters. A tremendous camaraderie exists among sailors, particularly on the water, which makes sailing — and the people who do it — very special.

What can US SAILING do for you?

US SAILING is committed to helping you discover and enjoy the beauty, relaxation, challenge and friendships of sailing. As part of this commitment we offer:

THE KEELBOAT CERTIFICATION SYSTEM with its various levels of training and certification:

- **Basic Keelboat.** To responsibly skipper and crew a simple daysailing keelboat in familiar waters in light to moderate wind and sea conditions.

- **Basic Cruising.** To responsibly skipper and crew an auxiliary powered cruising sailboat during daylight hours within sight of land in moderate wind and sea conditions.

- **Bareboat Cruising**. To responsibly skipper, crew or bareboat charter an inboard auxiliary powered cruising sailboat within sight of land to a port or an anchorage during daylight hours in moderate to strong wind and sea conditions.

- **Coastal Navigation.** To properly use traditional navigation techniques and electronic navigation for near coastal passage making.

- **Coastal Passage Making.** To responsibly skipper and crew an inboard auxiliary powered cruising sailboat for coastal or offshore passages in strong to heavy conditions, including zero visibility and nighttime, in unfamiliar waters out of sight of land.

- **Celestial Navigation.** To navigate using celestial techniques and integrating celestial with traditional navigation.

- **Offshore Passage Making.** To responsibly skipper and crew an inboard auxiliary powered cruising sailboat to any destination worldwide.

Plus many other useful services:

US SAILING certified instructors help you achieve new skills and knowledge using up to date and safe methods.

Course materials, including this book, presented in a highly visual format to help you gain competency and confidence in your sailing skills and knowledge.

The Official Logbook of Sailing, recognized nationally and internationally, to document your US SAILING certifications and experience and use as a passport to chartering boats locally and worldwide.

A national database so charter companies can confirm your sailing credentials.

A list of sailing schools that use US SAILING certified instructors and US SAILING course materials.

US SAILING Safety-at-Sea seminars.

U.S. Coast Guard recognition of the completion of a safe boating course, often one of the requirements for licensing.

Racing Rules and handicap rating systems.

US SAILING membership making you a part of the National Governing Body for the Sport of Sailing and the recipient of a free one-year subscription to a major sailing magazine as well as discounts on products and services.

The Keelboat Certification System was developed by volunteers representing sailing schools, charter companies, sailors, and the sailing industry.

—Welcome aboard!

Notes

A special acknowledgement to Sail America

US SAILING would like to thank Sail America for their continuing support of quality sailing instruction and the generous grant they provided to help publish this book.

Sail America (originally A.S.A.P.) was formed in 1990 to represent all segments of the sailing industry — from boatbuilders to sailing schools — with the mission of stimulating public interest in sailing and expanding the sailing market in the US.

With this in mind, Sail America creates and manages its own boat shows and then reinvests the money earned from the shows to benefit the sport of sailing. In 1991, Sail America launched SAIL EXPO Atlantic City which is now an established annual show. Since then they have added SAIL EXPO St. Petersburg in 1995 and PACIFIC SAIL EXPO in 1997.

As a result, Sail America has been able to reinvest a substantial percentage of show earnings to benefit sailing through several important programs including:

- Grants to improve the quality of sailing instruction and training (i.e., funding this book)

- A grant for the "Class Afloat" program to stimulate awareness of junior and senior high school students in sailing

- Grants to provide sailing equipment and promotional materials to associations that benefit physically challenged sailors.

Sail America's mission is to promote the growth of sailing as a sport, an industry, and a way of life in harmony with the environment. For more information on Sail America, please call (401) 841-0900.

Sail America